One Hundred

BIBLE STORIES

In the Words of Holy Scripture

*Based on the New International Version
With Colored Illustrations, Scripture Passages,
Questions, and Explanatory Notes*

CONCORDIA PUBLISHING HOUSE · SAINT LOUIS

1 2 3 4 5 6 7 8 9 10   14 13 12 11 10 09 08 07 06 05

Contents

Preface

The Old Testament

The New Testament

The Public Ministry of Christ (about A.D. 29 to 33)

Parables of the Savior (about A.D. 29 to 33)

The Passion and Death of Christ (about A.D. 33)

The Glorified Christ (about A.D. 33)

Preface

For the past 50 years, *One Hundred Bible Stories* has introduced students and families to the truth and beauty of God's Word. Through the actual words of Holy Scripture and distinctive artwork, the history of God and His people comes alive on every page, drawing us into *the* story of God's grace revealed in Jesus Christ.

This new, revised edition of *One Hundred Bible Stories* continues the tradition by excerpting the key passages of Scripture in the New International Version and presenting fresh, colorful artwork for each story. The stories contain only the essentials; for the complete text, refer to the references in the Table of Contents.

As with previous editions, the stories have been chosen for children ages 9 and above. In general, the format remains the same, although a new section, "For Reflection," has been added for application of the story to our lives as God's chosen people in Christ.

The book is ideal for day school and Sunday school classrooms, for confirmation and midweek programs, for home schooling, and for family devotions.

In outline, the main features are as follows:
1. Fifty Old Testament and fifty New Testament stories.
2. A story every other page, with artwork opposite the page.
3. Explanatory notes for difficult words and concepts.
4. A caption for each picture, designed to highlight the central truth.
5. "For Reflection" questions, suitable for family devotions and discussions.
6. "Words to Remember," a memory verse to reinforce the meaning of the story.

Parents and teachers will welcome the format and content of *One Hundred Bible Stories*. In a world characterized by busy schedules and little time for reading and reflecting on God's Word, this new edition provides a regular, enjoyable study of key narratives in Holy Scripture.

"Nuggets from the inexhaustible gold mine of the Scriptures." These words from the original Foreword still describe *One Hundred Bible Stories*. We pray that God will bless you as you read and study His Word, and that He will fulfill His purpose to use the Holy Scriptures to "make you wise for salvation through faith in Christ Jesus" (2 Timothy 3:15).

The Creation: The First to the Fourth Day

Genesis 1

In the beginning God created[1] the heavens and the earth.

Now the earth was formless and empty, darkness was over the surface of the deep, and the Spirit of God[2] was hovering over the waters. And God said, "Let there be light," and there was light. God saw that the light was good, and He separated the light from the darkness. God called the light "day," and the darkness He called "night." And there was evening, and there was morning—the first day.

And God said, "Let there be an expanse between the waters to separate waters from water."[3] And it was so. God called the expanse "sky." And there was evening, and there was morning—the second day.

And God said, "Let the water under the sky be gathered to one place, and let dry ground appear." And it was so. God called the dry ground "land," and the gathered waters He called "seas." And God saw that it was good. Then God said, "Let the land produce vegetation:[4] seed-bearing plants and trees on the land that bear fruit with seed in it, according to their various kinds." And it was so. The land produced vegetation: plants bearing seed according to their kinds and trees bearing fruit with seed in it according to their kinds. And God saw that it was good. And there was evening, and there was morning—the third day.

And God said, "Let there be lights in the expanse of the sky to separate the day from the night, and to give light on the earth." And it was so. God made two great lights—the greater light[5] to govern the day and the lesser light[6] to govern the night. He also made the stars. God set them in the expanse of the sky to give light on the earth. And God saw that it was good. And there was evening, and there was morning—the fourth day.

Explanatory Notes

[1]Made out of nothing. [2]Holy Spirit. [3]To separate water on earth from water in the atmosphere. [4]Green plant life for food. [5]Sun. [6]Moon.

God said, "Let there be light."

For Reflection
1. What does the creation tell us about the Creator?
2. What evidence of the effects of sin do you see in the natural world around you?
3. Another way God showed His power was in sending Jesus to live, die, and rise again for the sins of the world. How can we show our love for Jesus in the way we care for all the things He has made for us?

Words to Remember
Our God is in heaven; He does whatever pleases Him. *Psalm 115:3*

The Creation: The Fifth to the Seventh Day

Genesis 1

And God said, "Let the water teem[1] with living creatures, and let birds fly above the earth across the expanse of the sky." So God created the great creatures of the sea and every living and moving thing with which the water teems, according to their kinds, and every winged bird according to its kind. And God saw that it was good. God blessed them and said, "Be fruitful and increase in number and fill the water in the seas, and let the birds increase on the earth." And there was evening, and there was morning—the fifth day.

And God said, "Let the land produce living creatures according to their kinds: livestock, creatures that move along the ground, and wild animals, each according to its kind." And it was so. And God saw that it was good.

Then God said, "Let Us[2] make man in Our image, in Our likeness[3], and let them rule over all the earth, and over all the creatures that move along the ground." So God created man in His own image, in the image of God He created him; male and female He created them. God blessed them and said to them, "Be fruitful and increase in number;[4] fill the earth and subdue[5] it. Rule over the fish of the sea and the birds of the air and over every living creature that moves on the ground." God saw all that He had made, and it was very good. And there was evening, and there was morning—the sixth day.

Thus the heavens and the earth were completed in all their vast array.[6] By the seventh day God had finished the work He had been doing; so on the seventh day He rested[7] from all His work.

And God blessed the seventh day and made it holy, because on it He rested from all the work of creating that He had done.

Explanatory Notes

[1]Be filled with. [2]The triune God—Father, Son and Holy Spirit. [3]Adam and Eve knew God as He wishes to be known, and they were righteous and holy, doing God's will. [4]These first parents were to have children, and through them become the parents of all people in the world. [5]Control it in order to take care of it. [6]Richness or beauty. [7]Stopped His creative work, since it was complete.

God saw that it was good.

For Reflection

1 List several ways God has blessed you through the animals He has made.
2. People are the creation God loved the most. He loved us so much that He sent Jesus to be our Savior and Friend. What special work does God give us to do for His honor and glory?
3. How do people show their love for God in the way they regard the day of rest set aside by Him?

Words to Remember

By faith we understand that the universe was formed at God's command. *Hebrews 11:3*

Adam and Eve in Paradise

Genesis 2

The LORD God formed[1] the man[2] from the dust[3] of the ground and breathed into his nostrils the breath of life, and the man became a living being.

Now the LORD God had planted a garden in Eden;[4] and there He put the man He had formed. And He made all kinds of trees grow out of the ground—trees that were pleasing to the eye and good for food. In the middle of the garden were the tree of life and the tree of the knowledge of good and evil. A river watering the garden flowed from Eden. The LORD God took the man and put him in the Garden of Eden to work it and take care of it.

And the LORD God commanded the man, "You are free to eat from any tree in the garden; but you must not eat from the tree of the knowledge of good and evil, for when you eat of it you will surely die."

The LORD God said, "It is not good for the man to be alone. I will make a helper suitable for him." So the LORD God caused the man to fall into a deep sleep; and while he was sleeping, He took one of the man's ribs and closed up the place with flesh. Then the LORD God made a woman from the rib He had taken out of the man, and He brought her to the man.

The man said, "This is now bone of my bones and flesh of my flesh; she shall be called 'woman,' for she was taken out of man." For this reason a man will leave his father and mother and be united to his wife, and they will become one flesh.[5]

The man and his wife were both naked, and they felt no shame.[6]

Explanatory Notes

[1]Shaped the man's body, like a potter shapes clay—this was the sixth day. [2]Adam. [3]Earth. [4]Also called Paradise. [5]Like one body, not to be separated—this was the first marriage. [6]Had no sin and therefore no evil thoughts.

Male and female He created them.

For Reflection
1. In what special way did God make the first man? the first woman?
2. Explain why marriage is a gift of God.
3. God gave Adam and Eve work to do in the Garden. How can we do our work in ways that show our love for Jesus?

Words to Remember
I praise You because I am fearfully and wonderfully made. *Psalm 139:14*

The Fall into Sin

Genesis 3

Now the serpent[1] was more crafty[2] than any of the wild animals the LORD God had made. He said to the woman, "Did God really say, 'You must not eat from any tree in the garden'?"[3]

The woman said to the serpent, "We may eat fruit from the trees in the garden, but God did say, 'You must not eat fruit from the tree that is in the middle of the garden,[4] and you must not touch it,[5] or you will die.'"

"You will not surely die," the serpent said to the woman. "For God knows that when you eat of it your eyes will be opened, and you will be like God, knowing good and evil.[6]"

When the woman saw that the fruit of the tree was good for food and pleasing to the eye, and also desirable for gaining wisdom,[7] she took some and ate it. She also gave some to her husband, who was with her, and he ate it.

Then the eyes of both of them were opened,[8] and they realized they were naked; so they sewed fig leaves together and made coverings for themselves.

Then the man and his wife heard the sound of the LORD God as He was walking in the garden in the cool of the day,[9] and they hid from the LORD God among the trees of the garden.[10]

Explanatory Notes

[1]The devil, disguised as a snake. [2]A liar, which Satan showed when, in speaking to the woman, he denied the truth of God's words. [3]This was to raise doubt in the woman's mind. [4]The tree of the knowledge of good and evil. [5]The woman does not give the exact words of God's command, which shows that the devil's influence was already working. [6]The devil's words are not true. [7]The woman wanted to be wise like God. [8]They realized they had sinned. [9]Evening. [10]They were afraid of God, fearing death which God had threatened for disobedience.

They hid from the LORD.

For Reflection

1. What consequences have come to you and to those around us as the result of Adam and Eve's sin?
2. How does the devil tempt us today? How has Jesus overcome sin and temptation for us?
3. After Adam and Eve sinned, they hid from God. Because we know Jesus as our Savior, we need never hide from God. What can we do instead?

Words to Remember

For the wages of sin is death, but the gift of God is eternal life in Christ Jesus our Lord. *Romans 6:23*

The Promise of the Savior

Genesis 3

But the LORD God called to the man, "Where are you?"

He answered, "I heard You in the garden, and I was afraid because I was naked; so I hid."

And He said, "Who told you that you were naked? Have you eaten from the tree that I commanded you not to eat from?"[1]

The man said, "The woman You put here with me—she gave me some fruit from the tree, and I ate it."[2]

Then the LORD God said to the woman, "What is this you have done?" The woman said, "The serpent deceived me, and I ate."

So the LORD God said to the serpent, "Because you have done this, cursed are you above all the livestock and all the wild animals! You will crawl on your belly and you will eat dust all the days of your life. And I will put enmity between you and the woman, and between your offspring and hers; He will crush your head,[3] and you will strike His heel."[4]

To the woman He said, "I will greatly increase your pains in childbearing; with pain you will give birth to children. Your desire will be for your husband, and he will rule over you."

To Adam He said, "Cursed is the ground because of you; through painful toil you will eat of it all the days of your life. It will produce thorns and thistles for you. By the sweat of your brow you will eat your food until you return to the ground, since from it you were taken; for dust you are and to dust you will return."

The LORD God made garments of skin for Adam and his wife and clothed them. After he drove the man out,[5] He placed on the east side of the Garden of Eden cherubim and a flaming sword flashing back and forth to guard the way to the tree of life.[6]

Explanatory Notes

[1]God knows everything. [2]The man blames God and the woman—anyone but himself—for his sin. [3]Destroy the devil's work. [4]Jesus had to suffer and die to break the power of the devil. [5]With his wife. [6]Paradise on earth was closed.

So that by His death He might destroy him who holds the power of death—that is, the devil (Hebrews 2:14).

For Reflection

1. What consequences of sin fell upon Eve? Adam? the serpent?
2. God told the serpent that the child of the woman would crush the head of the serpent. What did Jesus do to crush the head of Satan?
3. What does it mean to you that Jesus has defeated the power of the devil?

Words to Remember

For just as through the disobedience of the one man the many were made sinners, so also through the obedience of the one man the many will be made righteous. *Romans 5:19*

Cain and Abel

Genesis 4

Adam named his wife Eve, because she would become the mother of all the living. Eve became pregnant and gave birth to Cain. Later she gave birth to his brother Abel. Abel kept flocks,[1] and Cain worked the soil.[2]

In the course of time Cain brought some of the fruits of the soil as an offering to the LORD. But Abel brought fat portions from some of the firstborn of his flock. The LORD looked with favor on Abel and his offering,[3] but on Cain and his offering He did not look with favor. So Cain was very angry, and his face was downcast.[4]

Then the LORD said to Cain, "Why are you angry? If you do what is right, will you not be accepted? But if you do not do what is right, sin is crouching at your door; it desires to have you, but you must master it."

Now Cain said to his brother Abel, "Let's go out to the field." And while they were in the field, Cain attacked his brother Abel and killed him.

Then the LORD said to Cain, "Where is your brother Abel?" "I don't know," he replied. "Am I my brother's keeper?"

The LORD said, "What have you done? Listen! Your brother's blood cries out to me from the ground. Now you are under a curse and driven from the ground, which opened its mouth to receive your brother's blood from your hand. When you work the ground, it will no longer yield its crops for you. You will be a restless wanderer[5] on the earth."

Cain said to the LORD, "My punishment is more than I can bear. Today you are driving me from the land, and I will be hidden from your presence; whoever finds me will kill me."

But the LORD put a mark on Cain so that no one who found him would kill him.

Explanatory Notes
[1] A shepherd. [2] A farmer. [3] Liked it. [4] Looked upset. [5] One who goes from place to place.

The LORD looked with favor on Abel and his offering.

For Reflection

1. Why do you suppose God told Cain, "Sin is crouching at your door; it desires to have you, but you must master it"?
2. How did God show His grace to Cain? How does He show His grace to us?
3. How can we show our love and trust in Jesus as our Savior in the way we treat our brothers, sisters, and friends? in the way we treat all others, including strangers?

Words to Remember

This is how we know what love is: Jesus Christ laid down his life for us. And we ought to lay down our lives for our brothers. *1 John 3:16*

From Adam to Noah

Genesis 5

When Adam had lived 130 years, he had a son in his own likeness, in his own image;[1] and he named him Seth. After Seth was born, Adam lived 800 years and had other sons and daughters. Altogether, Adam lived 930 years, and then he died.[2]

Seth became the father of Enosh, and had other sons and daughters. Altogether, Seth lived 912 years. At that time men began to call on the name of the LORD.[3]

Enosh became the father of Kenan, and had other sons and daughters. Altogether, Enosh lived 905 years.

Kenan became the father of Mahalalel, and had other sons and daughters. Altogether, Kenan lived 910 years.

Mahalalel became the father of Jared, and had other sons and daughters. Altogether, Mahalalel lived 895 years.

Jared became the father of Enoch, and had other sons and daughters. Altogether, Jared lived 962 years.

Enoch became the father of Methuselah, and had other sons and daughters. Altogether, Enoch lived 365 years. Enoch walked with God; then he was no more,[4] because God took him away.

Methuselah became the father of Lamech, and had other sons and daughters. Altogether, Methuselah lived 969 years.

Lamech became the father of Noah and other sons and daughters. Altogether, Lamech lived 777 years.

After Noah was 500 years old, he became the father of Shem, Ham and Japheth.

Explanatory Notes

[1]Sinful, like Adam, not after the image of God. [2]As God had foretold. Likewise, all after him would die. [3]Began public worship. [4]Was no longer seen; he was taken to the presence of God without experiencing death.

Call on the name of the LORD.

For Reflection

1. Calling on the name of the Lord refers to public worship. During whose lifetime did public worship begin?
2. Why is it a privilege to "call on the name of the Lord" in public worship?
3. Enoch went to heaven without dying. The Bible says he "walked with God." Because of Jesus we need not be afraid of death. Explain.

Words to Remember

And everyone who calls on the name of the LORD will be saved. *Joel 2:32*

The Flood

Genesis 6–9

When men began to increase in number on the earth the LORD saw how great man's wickedness on the earth had become. The LORD was grieved that He had made man on the earth, and His heart was filled with pain. So He said, "I will wipe mankind from the face of the earth for I am grieved that I have made them."

But Noah found favor in the eyes of the LORD. Noah was a righteous man, and he walked with God. So God said to Noah, "I am going to put an end to all people, for the earth is filled with violence because of them. So make yourself an ark.[1] I am going to bring floodwaters on the earth. Everything on earth will perish, but I will establish My covenant[2] with you, and you will enter the ark—you and your sons and your wife and your sons' wives with you. You are to bring into the ark two of all living creatures, male and female, to keep them alive with you. You are to take every kind of food that is to be eaten for you and for them." Noah did everything just as God commanded him. Then the Lord shut him in.

On that day all the springs of the great deep[3] burst forth, and the floodgates of the heavens were opened.[4] And rain fell on the earth forty days and forty nights. The waters rose and increased greatly on the earth, and the ark floated on the surface of the water. All the high mountains were covered. Every living thing on the face of the earth was wiped out.

The waters flooded the earth for a hundred and fifty days. But God remembered Noah, and He sent a wind over the earth, and the waters receded. The ark came to rest on the mountains of Ararat. The waters continued to recede until the earth was completely dry.

Then God said to Noah, "Come out of the ark." So Noah came out, together with his sons and his wife and his sons' wives. All the animals came out of the ark, one kind after another. Then Noah built an altar to the LORD and he sacrificed burnt offerings on it.

God blessed Noah and his sons, saying to them, "Be fruitful and increase in number and fill the earth. I now establish My covenant with you and with your descendants after you: Never again will there be a flood to destroy the earth. I have set My rainbow in the clouds, and it will be the sign of the covenant between Me and the earth."

Explanatory Notes

[1]Boat. [2]A solemn pledge or agreement, often sealed and confirmed with a sign. [3]Water shut up in the earth. [4]It rained as never before or after.

"I have set My rainbow in the clouds, and it will be the sign of the covenant between Me and the earth."

For Reflection

1. What does the Flood remind us about God's attitude toward sin?
2. The rainbow reminds us that God keeps His promise. What promise came true when Jesus came to earth to live, die, and rise again?
3. How does Noah's ark symbolize the church?

Words to Remember

Baptism, which this prefigured, now saves you—not as a removal of dirt from the body, but as an appeal to God for a good conscience, through the resurrection of Jesus Christ. *1 Peter 3:21 NRSV*

The Tower of Babel[1]

Genesis 11

Noah's sons, according to their lines of descent, within their nations spread out over the earth after the flood. The whole world had one language and a common speech.[2]

As men moved eastward, they found a plain and settled there. They said to each other, "Come, let's make bricks and bake[3] them thoroughly." They used brick instead of stone, and tar for mortar.

Then they said, "Come, let us build ourselves a city, with a tower that reaches to the heavens, so that we may make a name[4] for ourselves and not be scattered over the face of the whole earth."

But the LORD came down to see the city and the tower that the men were building. He said, "If as one people speaking the same language they have begun to do this, then nothing they plan to do will be impossible for them. Come, let us go down and confuse their language so they will not understand each other."[5]

So the LORD scattered them from there over all the earth, and they stopped building the city. That is why it was called Babel—because there the LORD confused the language of the whole world. From there the LORD scattered them over the face of the whole earth.

Explanatory Notes

[1]Meaning confusion. [2]With only one language, everyone could understand one another and speak to one another. [3]They heated the bricks made of clay until they were as hard as stone. [4]They were proud and wanted fame and honor; the Flood had not destroyed sin. [5]Without a common language, joint effort became impossible.

"Let us build ... so that we may make a name for ourselves."

For Reflection
1. Why did the people want to build a tower?
2. How did the many languages of the world come into being?
3. God became angry with the people for trying to make a name for *themselves*, by their own doing. What name has God given us, by His doing?

Words to Remember

He has performed mighty deeds with His arm; He has scattered those who are proud in their inmost thoughts. *Luke 1:51*

The Call of Abram[1]

Genesis 12

The LORD said to Abram, "Leave your country and your father's household and go to the land I will show you. I will make you into a great nation and I will bless you; I will make your name great, and you will be a blessing; and all peoples on earth will be blessed through you."[2]

So Abram left, as the LORD had told him. He took his wife Sarai, and his nephew Lot, and they set out for the land of Canaan, and they arrived there. The LORD appeared to Abram and said, "To your offspring[3] I will give this land." So he built an altar there to the LORD, and called on His name.[4]

Now Lot, who was moving about with Abram, also had flocks and herds and tents. But the land could not support them while they stayed together, for their possessions were so great. So the two men parted company: Abram lived in the land of Canaan, while Lot lived among the cities of the plain and pitched his tents near Sodom. But the men of Sodom were wicked and were sinning greatly against the LORD.

After this, the word of the LORD came to Abram in a vision: "Do not be afraid, Abram. I am your shield,[5] your very great reward."[6]

But Abram said, "O Sovereign LORD, what can You give me since I remain childless?"

He took him outside and said, "Look up at the heavens and count the stars—if indeed you can count them." Then He said to him, "So shall your offspring be." Abram believed the LORD, and He credited it to him as righteousness.[7]

When Abram was ninety-nine years old, the LORD appeared to him and said, "I am God Almighty; walk before Me[8] and be blameless.[9] No longer will you be called Abram; your name will be Abraham, for I have made you a father of many nations. I will establish My covenant as an everlasting covenant to be your God and the God of your descendants after you."

Explanatory Notes

[1]A descendant of Shem. [2]In the Savior. [3]Children and children's children. [4]Worshiped the Lord with his family and servants. [5]Protector. [6]Having God, Abram had everything. [7]Abram knew God to be his Savior; God forgave his sins, and therefore he was just and holy in the sight of God. [8]Walk in the fear of God. [9]Lead a holy life.

"Look up at the heavens and count the stars ... so shall your offspring be."

For Reflection

1. How did Abraham show he loved God in the way he treated Lot?
2. When God told Abraham that all people would be blessed through him, God was referring to Jesus, who would be born as a descendant of Abraham. How are all people blessed through Jesus?
3. In what ways can you bless others because you know Jesus as your Savior?

Words to Remember

By faith Abraham, when called to go to a place he would later receive as his inheritance, obeyed and went, even though he did not know where he was going. *Hebrews 11:8*

The Promise of Isaac

Genesis 18

The LORD appeared to Abraham while he was sitting at the entrance to his tent in the heat of the day.[1] Abraham looked up and saw three men standing nearby.[2] When he saw them, he hurried from the entrance of his tent to meet them and bowed low to the ground. He said, "If I have found favor in your eyes, my lord, do not pass your servant by. Let me get you something to eat, so you can be refreshed and then go on your way."

"Very well," they answered, "do as you say."

So Abraham hurried into the tent to Sarah. "Quick," he said, "get three seahs[3] of fine flour and knead it and bake some bread." Then he ran to the herd and selected a choice, tender calf and gave it to a servant, who hurried to prepare it. He then brought some curds[4] and milk and the calf that had been prepared, and set these before them. While they ate, he stood near them under a tree.

"Where is your wife Sarah?" they asked him.

"There, in the tent," he said.

Then the LORD said, "I will surely return to you about this time next year, and Sarah your wife will have a son."

Now Sarah was listening at the entrance to the tent, which was behind Him. Abraham and Sarah were already old and well advanced in years, and Sarah was past the age of childbearing. So Sarah laughed to herself.

Then the LORD said to Abraham, "Why did Sarah laugh? Is anything too hard for the LORD? I will return to you at the appointed time next year and Sarah will have a son."

Sarah was afraid, so she lied and said, "I did not laugh."

But He said, "Yes, you did laugh."

Explanatory Notes
[1]Noon. [2]The Lord and two angels. [3]About 20 quarts. [4]Butter.

"Sarah will have a son."

For Reflection

1. Who were Abraham's visitors? Why did Sarah laugh at their message?
2. Abraham shared a special meal with the Lord and the angels. What special meal do God's people share as part of a worship service? What makes this meal so special?
3. Is anything too hard for the Lord? Why or why not?

Words to Remember

"God is not a man, that He should lie, nor a son of man, that He should change His mind. Does He speak and then not act? Does He promise and not fulfill?" *Numbers 23:19*

Sodom and Gomorrah

Genesis 19

The two angels[1] arrived at Sodom in the evening, and Lot was sitting in the gateway of the city. When he saw them, he got up to meet them and they went with him and entered his house. He prepared a meal for them, and they ate.

Before they had gone to bed, all the men of the city of Sodom—both young and old—surrounded the house. They called to Lot, "Where are the men who came to you tonight? Bring them out to us so that we can have sex with them."

Lot went outside to meet them and shut the door behind him and said, "No, my friends. Don't do this wicked thing."

They said, "This fellow came here as an alien,[2] and now he wants to play the judge!"[3] They kept bringing pressure on Lot[4] and moved forward to break down the door. But the men[5] inside reached out and pulled Lot back into the house and shut the door. Then they struck the men who were at the door with blindness.

The two men said to Lot, "Do you have anyone else in the city who belongs to you? Get them out of here, because the LORD has sent us to destroy it." So Lot went out and spoke to his sons-in-law, but they thought he was joking.

With the coming of dawn, the angels urged Lot, saying, "Hurry! Take your wife and your two daughters, or you will be swept away when the city is punished. Flee for your lives! Don't look back!"

Then the LORD rained down burning sulfur on Sodom and Gomorrah. Thus He overthrew[6] those cities and the entire plain, including all those living in the cities—and also the vegetation in the land. But Lot's wife looked back, and she became a pillar of salt.

Explanatory Notes

[1]The same ones that visited Abraham. [2]Foreigner or outsider. [3]Pass judgement on them. [4]Tried to force him. [5]The angels. [6]Destroyed.

The Lord rained down burning sulfur.

For Reflection
1. Even in the act of destroying the wicked cities of Sodom and Gomorrah, God was at work saving His people. Explain.
2. How does God protect you from evil?
3. The destruction of Sodom and Gomorrah reminds us of the final destruction awaiting all the wicked. Why can all who trust in Jesus as their Savior look forward to their eternal future with confidence?

Words to Remember
The Lord will rescue me from every evil attack and will bring me safely to His heavenly kingdom. To Him be glory for ever and ever. Amen. *2 Timothy 4:18*

The Offering of Isaac

Genesis 22

Sarah became pregnant and bore a son to Abraham in his old age. Abraham gave the name Isaac to the son Sarah bore him and circumcised him.[1]

Some time later God tested Abraham. He said to him, "Take your son, your only son, Isaac, whom you love, and go to the region of Moriah. Sacrifice him there as a burnt offering."

Early the next morning Abraham got up, took with him his son Isaac and enough wood for the burnt offering, and set out. On the third day Abraham looked up and saw the place in the distance. He took the wood for the burnt offering and placed it on his son Isaac, and he himself carried the fire[2] and the knife.

As the two of them went on together, Isaac spoke up and said, "Father? The fire and wood are here, but where is the lamb for the burnt offering?"

Abraham answered, "God Himself will provide the lamb for the burnt offering, my son."

When they reached the place God had told him about, Abraham built an altar there and arranged the wood on it. He bound his son Isaac and laid him on the altar, on top of the wood. Then he reached out his hand and took the knife to slay his son.

But the angel of the LORD called out to him from heaven, "Abraham! Do not lay a hand on the boy. Now I know that you fear God, because you have not withheld from Me your son, your only son." Abraham looked up and there in a thicket[3] he saw a ram[4] caught by its horns. He sacrificed it as a burnt offering instead of his son.

The angel of the LORD called to Abraham from heaven a second time and said, "I swear by Myself, declares the LORD, that because you have done this, I will surely bless you and make your descendants as numerous as the stars in the sky, and through your offspring all nations on earth will be blessed, because you have obeyed Me."

Explanatory Notes
[1]On the eighth day, as God commanded. [2]Carried live coals in a vessel. [3]Bushes. [4]Male sheep.

"Now I know that you fear God."

For Reflection
1. What did Abraham show about his love for God in his willingness to sacrifice his son?
2. Which other Father willingly allowed His Son to give His life as a sacrifice? What does this sacrifice mean to you?
3. Tell what it means to fear, love, and trust in God above all things.

Words to Remember

He who did not spare His own Son, but gave Him up for us all—how will He not also, along with Him, graciously give us all things? *Romans 8:32*

Isaac and His Family

Genesis 27

Isaac was forty years old when he married Rebekah. Rebekah became pregnant, and gave birth to twin boys. The first to come out was red, and his whole body was like a hairy garment; so they named him Esau. His brother was named Jacob. Isaac loved Esau, but Rebekah loved Jacob.

When Isaac was old and his eyes were so weak that he could no longer see, he called for Esau and said to him, "Prepare me the kind of tasty food I like and bring it to me to eat, so that I may give you my blessing."

Now Rebekah was listening as Isaac spoke to Esau. She said to Jacob, "Go out to the flock and bring me two choice young goats, so I can prepare some tasty food for your father. Then take it to your father to eat, so that he may give you his blessing."[1]

So he went and got them and brought them to his mother, and she prepared some tasty food. Then Rebekah took the best clothes of Esau and put them on Jacob. She also covered his hands and the smooth part of his neck with the goatskins. He went to his father and said, "My father."

"Yes, my son," he answered. "Who is it?"

Jacob said, "I am Esau. Please sit up and eat some of my game [2] so that you may give me your blessing."

Then Isaac said to Jacob, "Come near so I can touch you, my son, to know whether you really are my son Esau or not." Isaac touched him and said, "The voice is the voice of Jacob, but the hands are the hands of Esau." He did not recognize him, for his hands were hairy like those of his brother Esau.

"Are you really my son Esau?" he asked. "I am," he replied. Then Isaac said to him, "Come here, my son, and kiss me."

So he went to him and kissed him. When Isaac caught the smell of his clothes, he blessed him and said, "May God give you of heaven's dew and of earth's richness … May nations serve you and peoples bow down to you. Be lord over your brothers. May those who curse you be cursed and those who bless you be blessed."

Explanatory Notes
[1] She knew Jacob was supposed to receive the blessing. [2] The meat Jacob prepared.

34

Isaac went out to meditate.

For Reflection
1. Why were the actions of Rebecca and Jacob wrong?
2. What does Jesus' life, death, and resurrection mean for us when we feel sorrow over our own lies and dishonest acts?
3. As children of God, we also receive a blessing from our Father. What blessing have we received from Him? How have we received it?

Words to Remember
By faith Isaac blessed Jacob and Esau in regard to their future. *Hebrews 11:20*

35

Jacob's Stairway

Genesis 28

Jacob had scarcely left his father's presence, when his brother Esau came in from hunting. His father asked him, "Who are you?" "I am your son," he answered, "your firstborn,[1] Esau." Isaac said, "Your brother came deceitfully and took your blessing." Esau said, "Bless me too, my father!" Then Esau wept aloud. Isaac answered him, "Your dwelling will be away from the earth's richness. You will live by the sword and you will serve your brother."[2]

Esau held a grudge against Jacob because of the blessing. He said to himself, "I will kill my brother Jacob." When Rebekah was told what Esau had said, she sent for Jacob and said to him, "Flee at once to my brother Laban in Haran." Isaac called for Jacob and said, "May God Almighty bless you and may He give you the blessing given to Abraham."

Jacob set out for Haran. When he reached a certain place, he stopped for the night. Taking one of the stones there, he put it under his head and lay down to sleep. He had a dream in which he saw a stairway resting on the earth, with its top reaching to heaven, and the angels of God were ascending[3] and descending[4] on it. There above it stood the LORD, and He said: "I am the LORD, the God of your father Abraham and the God of Isaac. I will give you and your descendants the land on which you are lying."

When Jacob awoke from his sleep, he thought, "How awesome is this place![5] This is none other than the house of God; this is the gate of heaven."

Jacob took the stone he had placed under his head and set it up as a pillar[6] and poured oil on top of it. He called that place Bethel. Then Jacob made a vow,[7] saying, "If God will be with me and will watch over me so that I return safely to my father's house, then the LORD will be my God and this stone will be God's house."

Explanatory Notes

[1]Esau had previously sold his birthright to Jacob; he had despised it. [2]Esau's descendants would live in need, defeat other nations, but serve Jacob's descendants. [3]Going up. [4]Going down. [5]God's presence filled Jacob with fear and reverence. [6]Marker. [7]A solemn promise.

"God will be with me and watch over me."

For Reflection
1. One sin often leads to another. Jacob tricked his brother out of his blessing. How did Esau respond?
2. Why do you think God gave Jacob the dream of the stairway to heaven with angels ascending and descending on it?
3. Jesus is the Son of God and Son of Man, on whom the angels ascend and descend. Explain.

Words to Remember

"I tell you the truth, you shall see heaven open, and the angels of God ascending and descending on the Son of Man." *John 1:51*

Jacob's Family

Genesis 37

Jacob went to Laban and served him fourteen years for his daughters Leah and Rachel; and after that he served him six more years for cattle; and Jacob grew exceedingly prosperous. Then the LORD said to Jacob, "Go back to the land of your fathers and to your relatives, and I will be with you." Then Jacob put his children and his wives on camels, and went to his father Isaac in the land of Canaan.

Jacob had twelve sons: Reuben, Simeon, Levi, Judah, Dan, Naphtali, Gad, Asher, Issachar, Zebulun, Joseph, and Benjamin.

Joseph, who was seventeen, was tending the flocks with his brothers, and he brought their father a bad report about them.[1] Now Israel[2] loved Joseph more than any of his other sons, because he had been born to him in his old age; and he made a richly ornamented[3] robe for him. When his brothers saw that their father loved him more than any of them, they hated him and could not speak a kind word to him.

Joseph had a dream, and when he told it to his brothers, they hated him all the more. He said to them, "Listen to this dream I had: We were binding sheaves[4] of grain out in the field when suddenly my sheaf rose and stood upright, while your sheaves gathered around mine and bowed down to it."

His brothers said to him, "Do you intend to reign over us?" And they hated him all the more.

Then he had another dream, and he told it to his brothers. "Listen," he said, "I had another dream, and this time the sun and moon and eleven stars were bowing down to me."

When he told his father as well as his brothers, his father rebuked him and said, "What is this dream you had? Will your mother and I and your brothers actually come and bow down to the ground before you?"

His brothers were jealous of him, but his father kept the matter in mind.[5]

Explanatory Notes
[1]Told him of their evil deeds. [2]Jacob. [3]Richly colored. [4]Bundles. [5]Remembered it.

Joseph had a dream, and ... told it to his brothers.

For Reflection

1. How was Joseph regarded by his father? by his brothers? Why did they regard him as they did?
2. What relationships trouble and concern you? What does Jesus' life, death, and resurrection mean to you as you think about those relationships?
3. Just as Joseph was Jacob's favorite child, we are favored in God's eyes. God gives us a "richly ornamented robe" too. (See verse in "Words to Remember.") What does this mean?

Words to Remember

I delight greatly in the LORD; my soul rejoices in my God. For He has clothed me, with garments of salvation and arrayed me in a robe of righteousness. *Isaiah 61:10*

Joseph and His Brothers

Genesis 37

Now Joseph's brothers had gone to graze their father's flocks near Shechem. Israel said to Joseph, "Go and see if all is well with your brothers and with the flocks, and bring word back to me."

Joseph went and found them near Dothan. But they saw him in the distance, and plotted to kill him. "Here comes that dreamer!" they said to each other. "Come now, let's kill him and say that a ferocious animal devoured him. Then we'll see what comes of his dreams." When Reuben heard this, he tried to rescue him from their hands. "Let's not take his life," he said. "Throw him into this cistern,[1] but don't lay a hand on him."

So when Joseph came to his brothers, they stripped him of his robe—the richly ornamented robe he was wearing—and threw him into the cistern. Now the cistern was empty; there was no water in it. As they sat down to eat their meal, they looked up and saw a caravan coming. Judah said to his brothers, "Come, let's sell our brother." His brothers agreed. So when the merchants came by, his brothers pulled Joseph up out of the cistern and sold him for twenty shekels of silver[2] to the Ishmaelites,[3] who took him to Egypt.

When Reuben returned to the cistern and saw that Joseph was not there, he tore his clothes. He went back to his brothers and said, "The boy isn't there! Where can I turn now?"[4] Then they got Joseph's robe, slaughtered a goat and dipped the robe in the blood. They took the ornamented robe back to their father and said, "We found this. Examine it to see whether it is your son's robe."

He recognized it and said, "It is my son's robe! Some ferocious animal has devoured him. Joseph has surely been torn to pieces." Then Jacob tore his clothes, put on sackcloth and mourned for his son many days. All his sons and daughters came to comfort him, but he refused to be comforted. "No," he said, "in mourning will I go down to the grave to my son."[5]

Explanatory Notes

[1] Hole or well. [2] The price of a young slave. [3] Also called Midianites. [4] As the oldest, he was responsible for Joseph's welfare. [5] He felt he would die of grief.

His brothers ... sold him for twenty shekels of silver.

For Reflection
1. Jacob's sons tricked him into thinking Joseph has been killed by a wild animal. Jacob also had at one time also tricked his father. Recall the incident.
2. The evil thoughts of Joseph's brothers led to evil actions. Explain.
3. Reuben intercedes for Joseph, and saves his life. Who has interceded for our lives? How?

Words to Remember

[Jesus] is able to save completely those who come to God through Him, because He always lives to intercede for them. *Hebrews 7:25*

Joseph Serves Pharaoh

Genesis 41

When years had passed, Pharaoh had a dream: He was standing by the Nile, when out of the river there came up seven cows, sleek and fat. After them, seven other cows, ugly and gaunt,[1] came up out of the Nile and ate up the seven sleek, fat cows. Then Pharaoh woke up. He fell asleep again and had a second dream: Seven heads of grain, healthy and good, were growing on a single stalk. After them, seven other heads of grain sprouted—thin and scorched by the east wind. The thin heads of grain swallowed up the seven healthy, full heads. Then Pharaoh woke up.

In the morning his mind was troubled, so he sent for all the magicians[2] of Egypt. Pharaoh told them his dreams, but no one could interpret them for him. Then Pharaoh sent for Joseph, and he was quickly brought before Pharaoh. Pharaoh said to Joseph, "I had a dream, and no one can interpret it. But I have heard it said that when you hear a dream you can interpret it."

"I cannot do it," Joseph replied to Pharaoh, "but God will give Pharaoh the answer he desires." Then Pharaoh told Joseph his dreams.

Joseph said, "The dreams of Pharaoh are one and the same. Seven years of great abundance are coming throughout the land of Egypt, but seven years of famine[3] will follow them. And now let Pharaoh look for a discerning[4] and wise man and put him in charge of the land of Egypt. Let Pharaoh appoint commissioners to take a fifth of the harvest of Egypt during the seven years of abundance. This food should be held in reserve[5] for the country, to be used during the seven years of famine."

Then Pharaoh said to Joseph, "Since God has made all this known to you, there is no one so discerning and wise as you. I hereby put you in charge of the whole land of Egypt."

Joseph collected all the food produced in those seven years of abundance in Egypt and stored it in the cities. Joseph stored up huge quantities of grain; it was so much that he stopped keeping records because it was beyond measure. The seven years of abundance in Egypt came to an end, and the seven years of famine began. There was famine in all the other lands, but in the whole land of Egypt there was food.

Explanatory Notes

[1]Very thin. [2]These people did supernatural things with the help of Satan. [3]General shortage of food. [4]Showing understanding and insight. [5]Storage.

Joseph stored up huge quantities of grain.

For Reflection
1. What dreams did Pharaoh dream? How did Joseph interpret them?
2. Joseph told Pharaoh that God would give him an answer of peace. How does Jesus bring peace to all who love and trust in Him?
3. God blessed Joseph abundantly. How does God abundantly bless all believers in Christ Jesus?

Words to Remember
The LORD upholds the righteous. *Psalm 37:17*

The Journeys of Joseph's Brothers

Genesis 42–43

When Jacob learned that there was grain in Egypt, he said to his sons, "I have heard that there is grain in Egypt. Go down there and buy some for us, so that we may live and not die." So ten of Joseph's brothers went down to buy grain from Egypt. Now Joseph was the governor of the land, the one who sold grain to all its people. So when Joseph's brothers arrived, they bowed down to him. Although Joseph recognized his brothers, they did not recognize him. He turned away from them and began to weep. He had Simeon taken from them and bound before their eyes. Then he gave orders to fill their bags with grain and they left.

Now the famine was still severe in the land. So when they had eaten all the grain they had brought from Egypt, their father said to them, "Go back and buy us a little more food."

But Judah said to him, "The man warned us solemnly,[1] 'You will not see my face again unless your brother is with you.' Send the boy along with me; you can hold me personally responsible for him."

Then their father Israel said to them, "If it must be, then do this. And may God Almighty grant you mercy before the man."

So the men hurried down to Egypt and presented themselves to Joseph. Joseph said to the steward of his house, "Take these men to my house; they are to eat with me at noon."

When Joseph saw his brother Benjamin, he asked, "Is this your youngest brother?" And he said, "God be gracious to you, my son."

Deeply moved at the sight of his brother, Joseph went into his private room and wept there. After he had washed his face, he came out and, controlling himself, said, "Serve the food." The men had been seated before him in the order of their ages, from the firstborn to the youngest; and they looked at each other in astonishment.[2] When portions were served to them, Benjamin's portion was five times as much as anyone else's.

Now Joseph gave these instructions to the steward of his house: "Fill the men's sacks with food, and put my cup, the silver one, in the mouth of the youngest one's sack." And he did as Joseph said.

Explanatory Notes
[1]Seriously. [2]They were amazed at being seated exactly according to their age.

Although Joseph recognized his brothers, they did not recognize him.

For Reflection
1. What occurrence astonished the brothers at the meal to which Joseph had invited them?
2. How had Judah assured Jacob regarding the safety of Benjamin?
3. How has Jesus taken personal responsibility for us before our Father in heaven?

Words to Remember
My command is this: Love each other as I have loved you. *John 15:12*

Joseph Makes Himself Known to His Brothers

Genesis 44–45

The men had not gone far from the city when Joseph said to his steward, "Go after those men, and say to them, 'Why have you repaid good with evil? Isn't this the cup my master drinks from? This is a wicked thing you have done.'" When he caught up with them, he repeated these words to them.

But they said to him, "Why would we steal silver or gold from your master's house? If any of your servants is found to have it, he will die; and the rest of us will become my lord's slaves."

Each of them quickly lowered his sack to the ground and opened it. And the cup was found in Benjamin's sack. At this, they tore their clothes,[1] and returned to the city.

Joseph said to them, "What is this you have done? The man who was found to have the cup will become my slave."

Then Judah went up to him and said: "Please, my lord, if the boy is not with us when I go back to my father, your servants will bring the gray head of our father down to the grave in sorrow. Your servant guaranteed the boy's safety to my father. Now then, please let your servant remain here as my lord's slave in place of the boy."

Then Joseph could no longer control himself, and he wept loudly. He said to his brothers, "I am Joseph! Is my father still living?" But his brothers were not able to answer him, because they were terrified at his presence.

Then Joseph said to his brothers, "Come close to me. I am your brother Joseph, the one you sold into Egypt! And now, do not be distressed and do not be angry with yourselves, because it was to save lives that God sent me ahead of you.[2] Now hurry back to my father and say to him, 'This is what your son Joseph says: God has made me lord of all Egypt. Come down to me; don't delay. I will provide for you.' And bring my father down here quickly." Then he threw his arms around his brother Benjamin and wept, and Benjamin embraced him, weeping. And he kissed all his brothers.

Explanatory Notes

[1]Tore their outer clothing to show their grief. [2]Joseph understood God's plan.

46

"Do not be distressed … God sent me ahead of you."

For Reflection

1. Judah volunteered to serve as a substitute for Benjamin. How does Judah remind us of Jesus?
2. Joseph made himself known to his brothers, adding that God was working in the events that had occurred to save their lives. Explain.
3. How does God make Himself known to us? Why is it important that He does?

Words to Remember

Bear with each other and forgive whatever grievances you may have against one another. Forgive as the Lord forgave you. *Colossians 3:13*

47

Jacob and Joseph Are Reunited

Genesis 46–50

Joseph gave them carts, and he also gave them provisions[1] for their journey. To each of them he gave new clothing, but to Benjamin he gave three hundred shekels of silver[2] and five sets of clothes. Then he sent his brothers away, and as they were leaving he said to them, "Don't quarrel on the way!"

So they went up out of Egypt and came to their father Jacob (Israel) in the land of Canaan. They told him, "Joseph is still alive! In fact, he is ruler of all Egypt." Jacob did not believe them. But when they told him everything Joseph had said to them, and when he saw the carts Joseph had sent to carry him back, the spirit of their father Jacob revived. And Israel said, "I'm convinced! My son Joseph is still alive. I will go and see him before I die."

So Israel set out with all that was his. Now Jacob sent Judah ahead of him to Joseph. Joseph had his chariot[3] made ready and went to meet his father. As soon as Joseph appeared before him, he threw his arms around his father and wept for a long time. Israel said to Joseph, "Now I am ready to die, since I have seen for myself that you are still alive." Then Joseph brought his father Jacob in and presented him before Pharaoh and Jacob blessed Pharaoh.

So Joseph settled his father and his brothers in Egypt and gave them property in the best part of the land. Joseph also provided his father and his brothers and all his father's household with food.

When the time drew near for Israel to die, he called for his sons and blessed them,[4] and was gathered to his people.[5] Then Jacob's sons did as he commanded and buried him near Mamre. When Joseph's brothers saw that their father was dead, they sent word to Joseph, saying, "Forgive your brothers the sins and the wrongs they committed in treating you so badly."

Joseph wept and said to them, "You intended to harm me, but God intended it for good. So then, don't be afraid. I will provide for you and your children." And he reassured them and spoke kindly to them.

Explanatory Notes

[1]Food for the brothers and their animals. [2]As a special sign of brotherly love. [3]A two-wheeled royal wagon. [4]Judah received the blessing of the Savior. Genesis 49:8–12. [5]He died.

He threw his arms around his father and wept.

For Reflection
1. What were Joseph's brothers afraid of after the death of their father?
2. Why are those who trust in Jesus as their Savior able to forgive others?
3. Read the verse in "Words to Remember." How did God work for good in Joseph's life? How does He work for good in our lives?

Words to Remember
And we know that in all things God works for the good of those who love Him, who have been called according to His purpose. *Romans 8:28*

The Birth of Moses

Exodus 1–2

Then a new king, who did not know about Joseph, came to power in Egypt. "Look," he said to his people, "the Israelites have become much too numerous for us. Come, we must deal shrewdly with them."[1]

So they put slave masters over them to oppress them with forced labor. But the more they were oppressed, the more they multiplied. Then Pharaoh gave this order to all his people: "Every [Hebrew] boy that is born you must throw into the Nile."

Now a Levite woman gave birth to a son. She hid him for three months. But when she could hide him no longer, she got a papyrus basket for him and coated it with tar and pitch.[2] Then she placed the child in it and put it among the reeds along the bank of the Nile. His sister stood at a distance to see what would happen to him.

Pharaoh's daughter went down to the Nile to bathe. She saw the basket among the reeds and sent her slave girl to get it. She opened it and saw the baby. He was crying, and she felt sorry for him. "This is one of the Hebrew babies," she said.

Then his sister asked Pharaoh's daughter, "Shall I go and get one of the Hebrew women to nurse the baby for you?"

"Go," she answered. And the girl went and got the baby's mother. Pharaoh's daughter said to her, "Take this baby and nurse him for me, and I will pay you." So the woman took the baby and nursed him. When the child grew older, she took him to Pharaoh's daughter and he became her son. She named him Moses.

One day, after Moses had grown up, he saw an Egyptian beating a Hebrew, one of his own people. He killed the Egyptian and hid him in the sand. When Pharaoh heard of this, he tried to kill Moses, but Moses fled from Pharaoh.

Explanatory Notes

[1] To keep them from becoming too powerful. [2] Black, sticky, waterproofing substance.

She saw the basket among the reeds and ... opened it and saw the baby.

For Reflection

1. Moses' mother saved Moses by placing him in a small boat—a basket coated with tar and pitch so that it would float. Compare Moses and Noah.
2. How did God protect Moses from danger? How does He protect us?
3. Moses was received as a baby in order to "save" God's people from slavery in Egypt. What other baby was born to save His people? How did He save us?

Words to Remember

By faith Moses, when he had grown up, refused to be known as the son of Pharaoh's daughter. He chose to be mistreated along with the people of God rather than to enjoy the pleasures of sin for a short time. *Hebrews 11:24–25*

The Call of Moses

Exodus 3–4

Now Moses was tending the flock of his father-in-law, and he led the flock to the far side of the desert and came to Horeb, the mountain of God. There the angel of the LORD appeared to him in flames of fire from within a bush. Moses saw that though the bush was on fire it did not burn up. God called to him from within the bush and said, "I have indeed seen the misery of my people in Egypt, and I am concerned about their suffering. So now, go. I am sending you to Pharaoh to bring my people the Israelites out of Egypt."

But Moses said to God, "Who am I, that I should go to Pharaoh and bring the Israelites out of Egypt?"

And God said, "I will be with you."

Moses answered, "What if they do not believe?"

Then the LORD said to him, "What is that in your hand?" "A staff," he replied. The LORD said, "Throw it on the ground." Moses threw it on the ground and it became a snake, and he ran from it. Then the LORD said to him, "Take it by the tail." So Moses reached out and took hold of the snake and it turned back into a staff in his hand.

Then the LORD said, "Put your hand inside your cloak." So Moses put his hand into his cloak, and when he took it out, it was leprous,[1] like snow. "Now put it back into your cloak," He said. So Moses put his hand back into his cloak, and when he took it out, it was restored, like the rest of his flesh. "If they do not believe these two signs or listen to you, take some water from the Nile and pour it on the dry ground. The water will become blood on the ground."

Moses said, "O Lord, I am slow of speech and tongue." The LORD said to him, "Go; I will help you speak and will teach you what to say." But Moses said, "O Lord, please send someone else to do it." Then the Lord's anger burned against Moses and he said, "What about your brother, Aaron? I know he can speak well. He will speak to the people for you." So Moses started back to Egypt. And he took the staff of God in his hand.

Explanatory Notes
[1]Leprosy is a destructive skin disease.

God appeared to Moses in flames of fire from within a bush.

For Reflection

1. Of what did God remind Moses when he asked, "Who am I, that I should go to Pharaoh and bring the Israelites out of Egypt?"
2. How did God equip and bless Moses for the work He had called him to do?
3. What gifts has God given to you to help you in your life?

Words to Remember

"You must go to everyone I send you to and say whatever I command you. Do not be afraid of them, for I am with you and will rescue you," declares the LORD. *Jeremiah 1:7–8*

The Passover[1]

Exodus 11–12

Afterward Moses and Aaron went to Pharaoh and said, "This is what the LORD, the God of Israel, says: 'Let my people go.'"

Pharaoh said, "Who is the LORD, that I should obey Him. I will not let Israel go."

Pharaoh's heart became hard and he would not listen to them. And the LORD brought nine plagues[2] upon Pharaoh and the Egyptians, but the LORD hardened Pharaoh's heart, and he was not willing to let them go.

Now the LORD had said to Moses, "I will bring one more plague on Pharaoh and on Egypt. After that, he will let you go. Tell the whole community of Israel to take a lamb without defect, one for each household, and slaughter it at twilight. Then they are to take some of the blood and put it on the sides and tops of the doorframes of the houses. That same night they are to eat the meat roasted over the fire, along with bitter herbs, and bread made without yeast. Do not leave any of it till morning. This is how you are to eat it: with your cloak tucked into your belt, your sandals on your feet and your staff in your hand.[3] Eat it in haste; it is the Lord's Passover. On that same night I will pass through Egypt and strike down every firstborn—both men and animals. The blood will be a sign for you on the houses where you are; and when I see the blood, I will pass over you. No destructive plague will touch you. This is a day you are to commemorate; for the generations to come you shall celebrate it as a festival to the LORD—a lasting ordinance."

The Israelites did just what the LORD commanded.

Explanatory Notes

[1]The Passover is a special meal (festival) that celebrates God's mighty rescue of His people from slavery in Egypt. It provides a preview and picture of God's salvation won by Christ in His death and resurrection. As the passover lamb was killed and its blood smeared on the Israelites' homes, so Christ was crucified— His blood was shed—for our forgiveness. As the Exodus passover brought Israel into a new life, Christ's resurrection brings us new life. [2]Terrible punishments of God. [3]They were to be ready to travel.

"When I see the blood, I will pass over you."

For Reflection
1. What was the Passover?
2. What were the Israelites to do on the evening before the Passover?
3. Why is Jesus called our Passover lamb?

Words to Remember
Christ, our Passover lamb, has been sacrificed. *1 Corinthians 5:7*

The Departure from Egypt

Exodus 12–14

At midnight the LORD struck down all the firstborn in Egypt, and there was loud wailing in Egypt, for there was not a house without someone dead.

During the night Pharaoh summoned Moses and Aaron and said, "Up! Leave my people!" The Egyptians urged the people to hurry and leave the country. "For otherwise," they said, "we will all die!"

The Israelites went up out of Egypt. There were about six hundred thousand men on foot, besides women and children. By day the LORD went ahead of them in a pillar of cloud to guide them on their way and by night in a pillar of fire to give them light.

When the king of Egypt was told that the people had fled, Pharaoh and his officials changed their minds and said, "What have we done? We have let the Israelites go and have lost their services!" So Pharaoh and his army pursued the Israelites and overtook them as they camped by the sea.

The Israelites were terrified and cried out to the LORD. Moses answered the people, "Do not be afraid. Stand firm and you will see the deliverance the LORD will bring you today. The Egyptians you see today you will never see again. The LORD will fight for you; you need only be still."

Then the angel of God, who had been traveling in front of Israel's army, withdrew and went behind them. The pillar of cloud also moved from in front and stood behind them, coming between the armies of Egypt and Israel. Then Moses stretched out his hand over the sea, and the waters were divided, and the Israelites went through the sea on dry ground, with a wall of water on their right and on their left.

The Egyptians followed them into the sea. The LORD looked down at the Egyptian army and threw it into confusion. He made the wheels of their chariots[1] come off so that they had difficulty driving. And the Egyptians said, "Let's get away from the Israelites! The LORD is fighting for them."

Then the LORD said to Moses, "Stretch out your hand over the sea." The water flowed back and covered the entire army of Pharaoh. Not one of them survived. Then Moses and the Israelites sang to the Lord.

Explanatory Notes
[1] Two-wheeled wagons.

"You will see the deliverance the Lord will bring you today."

For Reflection

1. What visual reminder of His presence among them did God give to His people?
2. God's salvation of His people during the exodus from Egypt points to the even more dramatic rescue God later provided all people in Jesus. Tell about how Jesus rescued you at Calvary.
3. Are there times when you feel like you're caught between the Egyptian army and the Red Sea? Why need you not be afraid?

Words to Remember

By faith the people passed through the Red Sea as on dry land; but when the Egyptians tried to do so, they were drowned. *Hebrews 11:29*

The Giving of the Law

Exodus 19–20

Then Moses led Israel from the Red Sea and they went into the Desert[1] of Shur. The whole community grumbled against Moses and Aaron and said to them, "You have brought us out into this desert to starve this entire assembly to death."

The LORD said to Moses, "I have heard the grumbling of the Israelites. Tell them, 'At twilight you will eat meat, and in the morning you will be filled with bread.'"

That evening quail came and covered the camp, and in the morning thin flakes like frost on the ground appeared on the desert floor. When the Israelites saw it, they said, "What is it?" Moses said to them, "It is the bread the LORD has given you to eat." The people of Israel called the bread manna. The Israelites ate manna forty years.

In the third month after the Israelites left Egypt, they entered the Desert of Sinai, and camped there in the desert in front of the mountain. And the LORD said to Moses, "Go to the people and consecrate[2] them today and tomorrow. Have them wash their clothes and be ready by the third day."

On the morning of the third day there was thunder and lightning, with a thick cloud over the mountain, and a very loud trumpet blast. Everyone in the camp trembled. Then Moses led the people out of the camp to meet with God, and they stood at the foot of the mountain. Mount Sinai was covered with smoke, because the LORD descended on it in fire. The whole mountain trembled violently, and the sound of the trumpet grew louder and louder. And God spoke all these words.[3]

The people stayed at a distance and said to Moses, "Speak to us yourself and we will listen. But do not have God speak to us or we will die."

Moses went up the mountain and stayed there forty days and forty nights. When the LORD finished speaking to Moses on Mount Sinai, He gave him the two tablets of the Testimony, the tablets of stone inscribed by the finger of God.

Explanatory Notes
[1]Wilderness. [2]Dedicate, prepare for worship. [3]The Ten Commandments.

The LORD gave him the two tablets of stone inscribed by the finger of God.

For Reflection
1. God demonstrated His presence with smoke, fire, and the trembling of the mountain. How does God come to us today?
2. Moses went up the mountain to speak with God on behalf of the people. In what way does Jesus speak to God on our behalf?
3. God sent manna and quail to help the Israelites by giving them food. He helped them by giving them the Law. Explain.

Words to Remember

You have not come to a mountain that can be touched and that is burning with fire; to darkness, gloom and storm; ... But you have come to Mount Zion, to the heavenly Jerusalem, the city of the living God. *Hebrews 12:18, 22*

59

The Golden Calf

Exodus 32; 34

When the people saw that Moses was so long in coming down from the mountain, they gathered around Aaron and said, "Come, make us gods who will go before us. As for this fellow Moses who brought us up out of Egypt, we don't know what has happened to him."

Aaron answered them, "Take off the gold earrings and bring them to me." He took what they handed him and made it into an idol cast in the shape of a calf.

Then they said, "These are your gods, O Israel, who brought you up out of Egypt." They sacrificed burnt offerings. Afterward they sat down to eat and drink and got up to indulge in revelry.[1]

Then the LORD said to Moses, "Go down, because your people have become corrupt. They are a stiff-necked[2] people."

Moses went down the mountain with the two tablets[3] of the Testimony[4] in his hands. The tablets were the work of God; the writing was the writing of God, engraved on the tablets. When Moses approached the camp and saw the calf and the dancing, his anger burned and he threw the tablets out of his hands, breaking them to pieces.

And he took the calf and burned it; then he ground it to powder, scattered it on the water and made the Israelites drink it. Then he stood at the entrance to the camp and said, "Whoever is for the LORD, come to me." And all the Levites rallied to him. The next day Moses said to the people, "You have committed a great sin. But now I will go up to the LORD; perhaps I can make atonement for your sin."

Moses chiseled out two stone tablets like the first ones and went up Mount Sinai. "O Lord, if I have found favor in your eyes," he said, "then go with us. Although this is a stiff-necked people, forgive our sin."

Then the LORD said: "I am making a covenant with you. Before all your people I will do wonders never before done in any nation in all the world."

When Moses came down from Mount Sinai with the two tablets of the Testimony in his hands, he was not aware that his face was radiant because he had spoken with the LORD.

Explanatory Notes

[1]Sinful worship practices, including immoral dancing. [2]Stubborn. [3]Slabs of stone. [4]The Ten Commandments.

He made an idol cast in the shape of a calf.

For Reflection

1. The people of Israel had time on their hands as they waited for Moses to come down from the mountain. How did they misuse their time?
2. What other gods do we sometimes worship?
3. Because of Jesus, why do we need not fear punishment over the commandments we have broken?

Words to Remember

Do not be idolaters, as some of them were; as it is written: "The people sat down to eat and drink and got up to indulge in pagan revelry." *1 Corinthians 10:7*

The Bronze Snake

Numbers 13–14; 21

The Israelites went out from the Desert of Sinai, and the LORD said to Moses, "Send some men to explore the land of Canaan."

So Moses sent them out. At the end of forty days they returned. They gave Moses this account: "We went into the land to which you sent us, and it does flow with milk and honey! But the people who live there are powerful. We can't attack those people; they are stronger than we are. We seemed like grasshoppers to them."

All the Israelites grumbled, "If only we had died in Egypt! Or in this desert! We should choose a leader and go back to Egypt." Joshua and Caleb, who were among those who had explored the land, tore their clothes and said, "The land is exceedingly good. If the LORD is pleased with us, He will lead us into that land. Only do not rebel against the LORD. And do not be afraid of the people, because the LORD is with us." But the whole assembly talked about stoning them.

The LORD said to Moses, "How long will these people treat Me with contempt? How long will they refuse to believe in Me?"

But Moses said to the LORD, "In accordance with Your great love, forgive the sin of these people, just as You have pardoned them from the time they left Egypt until now."

The LORD replied, "I have forgiven them, as you asked. Nevertheless, as surely as I live, no one who has treated me with contempt will ever see the land I promised to their forefathers. So tell them, 'Not one of you will enter the land except Caleb and Joshua. As for your children, I will bring them in to enjoy the land you have rejected. Your children will be shepherds here for forty years;[1] and you will know what it is like to have Me against you.'"

When Moses reported this to all the Israelites, they mourned bitterly. Then the LORD sent venomous snakes among them. Moses prayed for the people and the LORD said to Moses, "Make a snake and put it up on a pole; anyone who is bitten can look at it and live." So Moses made a bronze snake and put it up on a pole. Then when anyone was bitten by a snake and looked at the bronze snake, he lived.

Explanatory Notes
[1] They will have to stay in the wilderness for 40 years.

"Anyone who is bitten can look at it and live."

For Reflection
1. How did Joshua and Caleb show their trust in God?
2. What happened because the people, except Joshua and Caleb, refused to trust in God?
3. How is Jesus like the bronze snake the Lord told Moses to lift up to save the Israelites?

Words to Remember
"Just as Moses lifted up the snake in the desert, so the Son of Man must be lifted up." *John 3:14*

Israel Enters Canaan

Deuteronomy 34; Joshua 1–5

Moses climbed Mount Nebo. There the LORD showed him the whole land. Then the LORD said to him, "This is the land I promised on oath to Abraham, Isaac and Jacob when I said, 'I will give it to your descendants.' I have let you see it with your eyes, but you will not cross over into it."

And Moses the servant of the LORD died. He[1] buried him, but to this day no one knows where his grave is. The Israelites grieved for Moses thirty days.

After the death of Moses, the LORD said to Joshua: "Now then, cross the Jordan River into the land I am about to give to the Israelites. Be strong and very courageous. Do not let this Book of the Law depart from your mouth; meditate[2] on it day and night. Then you will be prosperous and successful. Have I not commanded you? Be strong and courageous. Do not be terrified; do not be discouraged, for the LORD your God will be with you wherever you go."

So Joshua ordered the officers of the people: "Get your supplies ready. Three days from now you will cross the Jordan."

When the people broke camp to cross the Jordan, the priests carrying the ark of the covenant[3] went ahead of them. As soon as the priests who carried the ark reached the Jordan and their feet touched the water's edge, the water from upstream stopped flowing. It piled up in a heap a great distance away, while the water flowing down to the Salt Sea[4] was completely cut off. So the people crossed over.

And the priests came up out of the river carrying the ark of the covenant of the LORD. No sooner had they set their feet on the dry ground than the waters of the Jordan returned to their place and ran at flood stage as before.

The day after the Passover, that very day, they ate some of the produce of the land: unleavened bread and roasted grain. The manna stopped the day after they ate this food from the land; there was no longer any manna for the Israelites, but they ate of the produce of Canaan.

Explanatory Notes

[1]God. [2]Read it and think about it. [3]A golden chest, carried on two poles that symbolized the throne of God; see Exodus 25:10–22. [4]Dead Sea.

The Lord said to Joshua: "Cross the Jordan River into the land I am about to give to the Israelites."

For Reflection

1. God told Joshua, "Be strong and very courageous. Do not let this Book of the Law depart from your mouth; meditate on it day and night." Apply God's words to your own life.
2. In what ways did God demonstrate His loving presence and care for His people?
3. The name *Joshua*, means "The Lord saves." Share how Jesus has saved you and now gives you courage as you live for Him.

Words to Remember

Blessed are they who keep His statutes and seek Him with all their heart. *Psalm 119:2*

The Conquest[1] of Canaan

Joshua 6–10

Now Jericho was tightly shut up because of the Israelites. Then the LORD said to Joshua, "See, I have delivered Jericho into your hands. March around the city once with all the armed men. Do this for six days. On the seventh day, march around the city seven times, with the priests blowing the trumpets. Have all the people give a loud shout; then the wall of the city will collapse."

And so they did. On the seventh day, they marched around the city seven times. The seventh time around, when the priests sounded the trumpet blast, Joshua commanded the people, "Shout!" The people shouted, and the wall collapsed; they took the city and destroyed it.

Then the five kings of the Amorites joined forces. The LORD said to Joshua, "Do not be afraid of them; I have given them into your hand."

Joshua took them by surprise. The LORD threw them into confusion before Israel. As they fled before Israel, the LORD hurled large hailstones down on them from the sky, and more of them died from the hailstones than were killed by the swords of the Israelites.

Joshua said to the LORD in the presence of Israel: "O sun, stand still over Gibeon, O moon, over the Valley of Aijalon." So the sun stood still, and the moon stopped, till the nation avenged itself[2] on its enemies. The sun stopped in the middle of the sky and delayed going down about a full day.

So the LORD gave Israel all the land He had sworn to give their forefathers, and they took possession of it and settled there. Not one of all the Lord's good promises to the house of Israel failed; every one was fulfilled.[3]

Explanatory Notes
[1]Capture of the land. [2]Took revenge. [3]God always keeps His promises.

The LORD said to Joshua, "See, I have delivered Jericho into your hands."

For Reflection

1. List the miracles God performed to help His people.
2. How did God keep the promise He made to the people of Israel?
3. How has God kept His promises to you?

Words to Remember

Your kingdom is an everlasting kingdom, and Your dominion endures through all generations. The LORD is faithful to all His promises and loving toward all He has made. *Psalm 145:13*

Gideon

Judges 6

Again the Israelites did evil in the eyes of the LORD, and He gave them into the hands of the Midianites. The Midianites camped on the land and ruined the crops and did not spare a living thing for Israel. The Israelites cried out to the LORD for help.

Gideon was threshing wheat in a winepress to keep it from the Midianites. When the angel of the LORD appeared to Gideon, he said, "Go and save Israel out of Midian's hand." Then the Spirit of the LORD came upon Gideon, and he blew a trumpet, and sent messengers. The people went up to meet him.

The LORD said to Gideon, "You have too many men for Me to deliver Midian into their hands. In order that Israel may not boast against Me that her own strength has saved her, announce now to the people, 'Anyone who trembles with fear may turn back.'" So twenty-two thousand men left, while ten thousand remained.

But the LORD said to Gideon, "There are still too many men. Take them down to the water. Separate those who lap the water with their tongues like a dog." Three hundred men lapped with their hands to their mouths. The LORD said to Gideon, "With the three hundred men I will save you."

The Midianites had settled in the valley as thick as locusts.[1] Dividing the three hundred men into three companies, Gideon placed trumpets and empty jars in the hands of all of them, with torches inside. "Watch me," he told them. "Follow my lead. When I and all who are with me blow our trumpets, then from all around the camp blow yours and shout, 'A sword for the LORD and for Gideon.'"

The three companies blew the trumpets and smashed the jars. They grasped the torches in their left hands and shouted. The LORD caused the men throughout the camp to turn on each other with their swords and they fled.

Explanatory Notes
[1]Grasshoppers.

"Shout, 'A sword for the Lord and for Gideon.'"

For Reflection
1. Why did the people of Israel cry out to the Lord?
2. For what reason did God want only 300 soldiers to go into battle against the Midianites?
3. Read the verse in "Words to Remember." After reading the story of Gideon, how do we know this passage is true?

Words to Remember
It is better to take refuge in the LORD than to trust in man. *Psalm 118:8*

Samson: Part 1

Judges 13–14

The angel of the LORD appeared to the wife of Manoah and said, "You are going to have a son. No razor may be used on his head, because the boy is to be a Nazirite,[1] and he will begin the deliverance of Israel from the hands of the Philistines." The woman gave birth to a boy and named him Samson. He grew and the LORD blessed him, and the Spirit of the LORD began to stir him.

Samson went down to Timnah and saw there a young Philistine woman. He said to his father and mother, "Get her for me as my wife." His father and mother replied, "Isn't there an acceptable woman among our people?" His parents did not know that this was from the LORD, who was seeking an occasion to confront[2] the Philistines.

Samson went down to Timnah together with his father and mother. Suddenly a young lion came roaring toward him. The Spirit of the LORD came upon him in power so that he tore the lion apart with his bare hands as he might have torn a young goat. Some time later, he turned aside to look at the lion's carcass. In it was a swarm of bees and some honey, which he scooped out with his hands and ate as he went along.

And Samson made a feast in Timnah, as was customary for bridegrooms. When he appeared, he was given thirty companions. "Let me tell you a riddle," Samson said to them. "If you can give me the answer within the seven days of the feast, I will give you thirty linen garments and thirty sets of clothes. Out of the eater, something to eat; out of the strong, something sweet."

For three days they could not give the answer. They said to Samson's wife, "Coax your husband into explaining the riddle for us, or we will burn you and your father's household." Then Samson's wife threw herself on him, sobbing. She cried the whole seven days of the feast. So on the seventh day he finally told her. She in turn explained the riddle to her people. On the seventh day the men of the town said to him, "What is sweeter than honey? What is stronger than a lion?"

Then the Spirit of the LORD came upon him in power. He went to Ashkelon, struck down thirty of their men, stripped them of their belongings and gave their clothes to those who had explained the riddle.

Explanatory Notes

[1] One dedicated to serve God. [2] Oppose or resist.

Suddenly a young lion came roaring toward him.

For Reflection
1. How do we know that God had a plan for Samson even before he was born?
2. Explain Samson's riddle and its meaning.
3. How do we know that God was with Samson? How do we know He is with us?

Words to Remember
God has said, "Never will I leave you; never will I forsake you." *Hebrews 13:5*

Samson: Part 2

Judges 15–16

The Philistines went up and camped in Judah. The men of Judah asked, "Why have you come to fight us?" "We have come to take Samson prisoner," they answered. So they bound him with two new ropes and led him up away. As he approached Lehi, the Philistines came toward him shouting. The Spirit of the LORD came upon him in power. The ropes on his arms became like charred flax, and the bindings dropped from his hands. Finding a fresh jawbone of a donkey, he struck down a thousand men.

Some time later, he fell in love with a woman whose name was Delilah. The rulers of the Philistines went to her and said, "See if you can lure him into showing you the secret of his great strength. Each one of us will give you eleven hundred shekels of silver."

So Delilah said to Samson, "Tell me the secret of your great strength and how you can subdued." With such nagging she prodded him day after day until he was tired to death. So he told her everything. "No razor has ever been used on my head," he said, "because I have been a Nazirite set apart to God. If my head were shaved, my strength would leave me."

Having put him to sleep on her lap, she called a man to shave off the seven braids of his hair. And his strength left him. But he did not know that the LORD had left him. Then the Philistines seized him, gouged out his eyes and took him down to Gaza to the prison.

Now the rulers of the Philistines assembled to offer a great sacrifice to Dagon their god. While they were in high spirits, they shouted, "Bring out Samson to entertain us." So they called Samson out of the prison, and he performed for them, and they stood him among the pillars.[1]

Now the temple was crowded with men and women, and on the roof were about three thousand men and women watching Samson perform. Then Samson prayed to the LORD, "O Sovereign LORD, remember me. Please strengthen me just once more." Then Samson reached toward the two central pillars on which the temple stood. He pushed with all his might, and down came the temple on the rulers and all the people in it. Thus he killed many more when he died than while he lived.

Explanatory Notes
[1]Posts on which the building rested.

Samson prayed, "O Sovereign L<small>ORD</small>, remember me."

For Reflection
1. What evidence can you give that Samson possessed great strength?
2. How did Samson lose his great strength?
3. What was the real source of Samson's strength? What is the source of our strength?

Words to Remember

If anyone serves, he should do it with the strength God provides, so that in all things God may be praised through Jesus Christ. *1 Peter 4:11*

73

Ruth

The Book of Ruth

There was a famine in the land. Elimelech, together with his wife, Naomi, and two sons, Mahlon and Kilion, went to live for a while in the country of Moab. Now Elimelech died, and Naomi was left with her two sons. They married Moabite women, one named Orpah and the other Ruth. After they had lived there about ten years, Mahlon and Kilion also died.

With her two daughters-in-law, Naomi left the place where she had been living and set out on the road that would take them back to the land of Judah. Then Naomi said to her two daughters-in-law, "Go back, each of you, to your mother's home." Orpah kissed her mother-in-law good-by, but Ruth clung to her. Ruth replied, "Where you go I will go, and where you stay I will stay. Your people will be my people and your God my God."

So the two women went on until they came to Bethlehem. Ruth went out and began to glean[1] in the fields behind the harvesters. As it turned out, she found herself working in a field belonging to Boaz, who was from the clan of Elimelech. So Boaz said to Ruth, "Don't go and glean in another field and don't go away from here. Stay here with my servant girls." At this she exclaimed, "Why have I found such favor in your eyes?" Boaz replied, "I've been told all about what you have done for your mother-in-law. May the LORD repay you for what you have done. May you be richly rewarded by the LORD, the God of Israel, under whose wings you have come to take refuge." Boaz gave orders to his men, "Even if she gathers among the sheaves, don't embarrass her. Rather, pull out some stalks for her from the bundles and leave them for her to pick up, and don't rebuke her."

Then Boaz announced to the elders and all the people, "I have bought all the property of Elimelech. I have also acquired Ruth, Mahlon's widow, as my wife." So Boaz took Ruth and she became his wife. She gave birth to a son, and they named him Obed. He was the father of Jesse, the father of David.

Explanatory Notes
[1]Gather leftover grain, as poor people were allowed to do.

Ruth went out and began to glean in the fields.

For Reflection

1. What might have made it difficult for Ruth to go with her mother-in-law to live in Bethlehem?

2. Many years later, Jesus would be born to a descendant of Ruth. How does Ruth's background remind us that Jesus came to be the Savior of all people?

3. Ruth's words to Naomi, "Where you go I will go, where you stay I will stay," are considered to be the ultimate example of friendship. What meaning do these words have when coming from our ultimate Friend?

Words to Remember

I will be with you; I will never leave you nor forsake you. *Joshua 1:5*

The Boy Samuel

1 Samuel 1–4

Elkanah had two wives; one was called Hannah and the other Peninnah. Peninnah had children, but Hannah had none. Hannah prayed to the LORD, saying, "O LORD Almighty, if You will only look upon Your servant and give her a son, then I will give him to the LORD for all the days of his life."

And the LORD remembered her. So in the course of time Hannah gave birth to a son. She named him Samuel. After he was weaned, she took the boy with her to the house of the LORD to Eli, the priest.

Now, Eli's sons were wicked men; they had no regard for the LORD. Eli, who was very old, heard about everything his sons were doing, but said nothing.

A man of God came to Eli and said to him, "Why do you honor your sons more than me? The LORD, the God of Israel, declares: 'Those who honor Me I will honor, but those who despise Me will be disdained.' Your two sons will both die on the same day."

The boy Samuel ministered before the LORD under Eli. One night, Samuel was lying down in the temple of the LORD. The LORD came, calling "Samuel! Samuel!" Then Samuel said, "Speak, for Your servant is listening." And the LORD said to Samuel: "See, I will carry out against Eli everything I spoke against his family."

Samuel was afraid to tell Eli the vision, but Eli called him and said, "What was it He said to you?" So Samuel told him everything. Then Eli said, "He is the LORD; let Him do what is good in His eyes."

Now the Israelites went out to fight against the Philistines. Eli's two sons were there with the ark of the covenant[1] of God. The Israelites were defeated; the ark of God was captured, and Eli's two sons died. That same day a man ran from the battle line and went to Eli and said, "Israel fled before the Philistines, and the army has suffered heavy losses. Also your two sons are dead and the ark of God has been captured." When he mentioned the ark of God, Eli fell backward off his chair by the side of the gate. His neck was broken and he died.

Explanatory Notes
[1]See Exodus 25:10–22 for a description.

Samuel ministered before the LORD under Eli.

For Reflection

1. How did Hannah show her gratefulness to God for the son He had given her?
2. Eli had spoiled his sons. He did not discipline them for their sins. What was the result?
3. God spoke to Eli. How does God speak to us today, telling us of our sin and of Jesus as our Savior from sin?

Words to Remember

For the LORD watches over the way of the righteous, but the way of the wicked will perish. *Psalm 1:6*

King Saul

1 Samuel 8–15

When Samuel grew old, all the elders of Israel gathered together and said to him, "Appoint a king to lead us, such as all the other nations have." But this displeased Samuel. The LORD told him: "Listen to all that the people are saying to you; it is not you they have rejected,[1] but they have rejected Me as their king."[2]

When Samuel brought all the tribes of Israel near, Saul son of Kish was chosen.[3] But when they looked for him, he was not to be found. So they inquired further of the LORD, and the LORD said, "He has hidden himself among the baggage." They ran and brought him out, and as he stood among the people they shouted, "Long live the king!"

Nahash the Ammonite went up and besieged Jabesh Gilead. The Spirit of God came upon Saul in power. Then the terror of the LORD fell on the people, and they turned out as one man, broke into the camp of the Ammonites, and slaughtered them.

Samuel said to Saul, "This is what the LORD Almighty says: 'Go, attack the Amalekites and totally destroy everything that belongs to them. Do not spare them.'" So Saul summoned the men and attacked the Amalekites. But Saul and the army spared the best of the sheep and cattle, everything that was good.

When Samuel reached him, Saul said, "The LORD bless you! I have carried out the Lord's instructions." But Samuel said, "What then is this bleating of sheep in my ears? What is this lowing of cattle that I hear?" Saul answered, "The soldiers brought them from the Amalekites; they spared the best of the sheep and cattle to sacrifice to the LORD your God, but we totally destroyed the rest."

"Why did you not obey the LORD?" said Samuel. "To obey is better than sacrifice.[4] Because you have rejected the word of the LORD, He has rejected you as king."

Explanatory Notes

[1]Turned away, refused, or discarded. [2]They no longer wanted God to rule them. [3]To be king. [4]No one should set God's Word aside.

"Because you have rejected the word of the LORD, He has rejected you as king."

For Reflection

1. Why was Samuel displeased at the people of Israel's desire for a king?
2. What did Saul do in disobedience to God?
3. Jesus desires to be king of our lives. What does Jesus, our King, invite us to do when we recognize that we have sinned?

Words to Remember

Now to the King eternal, immortal, invisible, the only God, be honor and glory for ever and ever. Amen. *1 Timothy 1:17*

David Is Chosen

1 Samuel 16–17

The LORD said to Samuel, "I am sending you to Jesse. I have chosen one of his sons to be king." So Samuel anointed David, son of Jesse, in the presence of his brothers, and from that day on the Spirit of the LORD came upon David.

Now the Spirit of the LORD had departed from Saul, and an evil spirit[1] tormented him. Then Saul sent messengers to Jesse and said, "Send me your son David." David came to Saul and whenever the evil spirit came upon Saul, David would take his harp and play. Then relief would come to Saul; he would feel better, and the evil spirit would leave him.

Now the Philistines gathered their forces for war. A champion named Goliath came out of the Philistine camp. He was over nine feet tall. He had a bronze helmet on his head and wore a coat of scale armor of bronze weighing five thousand shekels.[2] His spear shaft was like a weaver's rod.[3]

Goliath stood and shouted to the ranks of Israel, "Choose a man and have him come down to me. If he is able to kill me, we will become your subjects;[4] but if I kill him, you will become our subjects and serve us." On hearing the Philistine's words, Saul and all the Israelites were dismayed and terrified. For forty days the Philistine came forward every morning and evening and took his stand.

David had left Saul to tend his father's sheep at Bethlehem. Now Jesse said to David, "Go to the camp and see how your brothers are. They are with Saul and the men of Israel, fighting against the Philistines."

Early in the morning David set out. He reached the camp, ran to the battle lines, and greeted his brothers. As he was talking with them, Goliath stepped out from his lines and shouted his usual defiance. David asked, "Who is this uncircumcised Philistine that he should defy the armies of the living God?"

What David said was overheard and reported to Saul, and Saul sent for him.

Explanatory Notes

[1]Leading him to despondency, jealousy, and violence. [2]About 125 pounds. [3]A round beam, four or five inches in diameter. [4]People who submit to another people's rule.

Samuel anointed David, son of Jesse.

For Reflection

1. Describe the evil Goliath and the threat he posed to the people of Israel.
2. We all have evil that threatens us and the lives we desire to live for Jesus. Give an example of some "Goliaths" you face.
3. The Israelites, on hearing Goliath's threatening words, were terrified. Why can we be like David, and live without fear?

Words to Remember

The LORD will keep you from all harm—He will watch over your life. *Psalm 121:7*

David and Goliath

1 Samuel 17

David said to Saul, "Your servant will go and fight this Philistine."

Saul replied, "You are not able to go out against Goliath and fight him; you are only a boy, and he has been a fighting man from his youth."

But David said to Saul, "The LORD will deliver me from the hand of this Philistine."

Saul said to David, "Go, and the LORD be with you." Then he dressed David in his own tunic. He put a coat of armor on him and a bronze helmet on his head.

David tried walking around. "I cannot go in these," he said to Saul, "because I am not used to them." So he took them off. Then he took his staff in his hand, chose five smooth stones from the stream, put them in the pouch of his shepherd's bag and, with his sling in his hand, approached the Philistine.

Goliath looked David over and said, "Am I a dog, that you come at me with sticks?"

David said to the Philistine, "You come against me with sword and spear and javelin, but I come against you in the name of the LORD Almighty, the God of the armies of Israel. This day the LORD will hand you over to me, and the whole world will know that there is a God in Israel."

Reaching into his bag and taking out a stone, he slung it and struck the Philistine. The stone sank into his forehead, and he fell facedown on the ground. David ran and stood over him. He took hold of the Philistine's sword and cut off Goliath's head. When the Philistines saw that their hero was dead, they turned and ran. Then the men of Israel and Judah pursued the Philistines and their dead were strewn along the road.

"I come against you in the name of the LORD Almighty."

For Reflection
1. Why was David able to defeat the giant Goliath?
2. What words of David show that he gave God the glory for his victory over Goliath, rather than seeking praise for himself?
3. What "giants" has Jesus overcome for you? What "giants" has Jesus enabled you to overcome?

Words to Remember

The LORD delights in those who fear Him, who put their hope in His unfailing love. *Psalm 147:11*

David's Fall and Repentance

2 Samuel 11–12

David sent Joab out with the king's men and the whole Israelite army. But David remained in Jerusalem.

One evening David walked around on the roof of the palace. He saw Bathsheba, the wife of Uriah, bathing. David sent messengers to get her. She came to him, and he slept with her. Then she went back home. The woman conceived and sent word to David, saying, "I am pregnant."

So David wrote a letter to Joab. In it he wrote, "Put Uriah in the front line where the fighting is fiercest. Then withdraw from him so he will be struck down and die." So Joab put Uriah at a place where he knew the strongest defenders were. When the men fought against Joab, some of the men in David's army fell; moreover, Uriah the Hittite died.

When Uriah's wife heard that her husband was dead, she mourned for him. After the time of mourning was over, David had her brought to his house, and she became his wife and bore him a son.

But the thing David had done displeased the LORD. The LORD sent Nathan to David. When he came to him, he said, "There were two men in a certain town, one rich and the other poor. The rich man had a very large number of sheep and cattle, but the poor man had nothing except one little ewe lamb he had bought. He raised it, and it grew up with him and his children. It shared his food, drank from his cup and even slept in his arms. Now a traveler came to the rich man, but the rich man refrained from taking one of his own sheep or cattle to prepare a meal for the traveler who had come to him. Instead, he took the ewe lamb that belonged to the poor man."

David burned with anger against the man and said to Nathan, "As surely as the LORD lives, the man who did this deserves to die!"

Then Nathan said to David, "You are the man! You struck down Uriah the Hittite with the sword of the Ammonites and took his wife."

Then David said to Nathan, "I have sinned against the LORD."

Nathan replied, "The LORD has taken away your sin. You are not going to die. But because by doing this you have made the enemies of the LORD show utter contempt,[1] the son born to you will die."

Explanatory Notes

[1]To mock, ridicule, say bad things about God.

"I have sinned against the LORD."

For Reflection

1. How did David respond when Nathan confronted him with his sin?
2. After David acknowledged his sin, what did Nathan say to him?
3. We deserve to die because of our sins. What has Jesus done for us that qualifies us to be forgiven instead?

Words to Remember

Have mercy on me, O God, according to Your unfailing love; according to Your great compassion blot out my transgressions. *Psalm 51:1*

Absalom's Rebellion

2 Samuel 14–18

In all Israel there was not a man so highly praised for his handsome appearance as Absalom, the son of David. From the top of his head to the sole of his foot there was no blemish in him. He would get up early and stand by the side of the road leading to the city gate. Whenever anyone came with a complaint to be placed before the king, Absalom would say to him, "Look, your claims are valid and proper, but there is no representative of the king to hear you. If only I were appointed judge in the land!" Also, whenever anyone approached him to bow down before him, Absalom would reach out his hand, take hold of him, and kiss him. So he stole the hearts of the men of Israel.

At the end of four years, Absalom said to the king, "Let me go to Hebron and fulfill a vow I made to the LORD." The king said to him, "Go in peace." So he went to Hebron. Then Absalom sent secret messengers throughout the tribes of Israel to say, "As soon as you hear the sound of the trumpets, then say, 'Absalom is king in Hebron.'" And so Absalom's following kept on increasing.

A messenger came and told David. Then David said to all who were with him, "Come! We must flee, or none of us will escape from Absalom. He will move quickly to overtake us."

Absalom and all the men of Israel came to Jerusalem, so David and all the people with him set out and crossed the Jordan. Absalom crossed the Jordan with all the men of Israel. The king commanded his captains, "Be gentle with the young man Absalom for my sake." The army marched into the field to fight Israel, and there the army of Israel was defeated by David's men.

Now Absalom was riding his mule, and as the mule went under the thick branches of a large oak, Absalom's head got caught in the tree. He was left hanging in midair, while the mule he was riding kept on going. Joab took three javelins in his hand and plunged them into Absalom's heart. And ten of Joab's armor-bearers surrounded Absalom, struck him and killed him. They took Absalom, threw him into a big pit in the forest and piled up a large heap of rocks over him.

When David heard that his son Absalom had died, he wept and said, "O my son Absalom! If only I had died instead of you—O Absalom my son, my son."

David said, "O my son Absalom! If only I had died instead of you."

For Reflection

1. How did Absalom sin against his father?
2. In what ways have you rebelled against your parents? against your Father in heaven?
3. David cried over his rebellious son Absalom, and wished he could have died in his place. What did our heavenly Father do for us in our rebellion against Him?

Words to Remember

But You are our Father, though Abraham does not know us or Israel acknowledge us; You, O LORD, are our Father, our Redeemer from of old is Your name. *Isaiah 63:16*

Solomon and the Temple

1 Kings 3–8

Solomon sat on the throne of his father David. He loved the LORD. The LORD appeared to Solomon in a dream, and God said, "Ask for whatever you want Me to give you."

Solomon answered, "O LORD, I am only a little child[1] and do not know how to carry out my duties. So give your servant a discerning heart to govern your people and to distinguish between right and wrong."

The Lord was pleased that Solomon had asked for this. So God said to him, "I will give you a wise and discerning heart. Moreover, I will give you what you have not asked for—both riches and honor. And if you walk in My ways, I will give you a long life."

Solomon began to build the temple of the LORD. He spent seven years building it. When all the work was finished all the men of Israel came together. The priests took up the ark of the Lord's covenant, to its place in the inner sanctuary of the temple, the Most Holy Place. When the priests withdrew from the Holy Place, the glory of the LORD filled the temple.

Then Solomon stood before the altar of the LORD in front of the whole assembly of Israel, spread out his hands toward heaven and said: "O LORD, God of Israel, the heavens, even the highest heaven, cannot contain You.[2] How much less this temple I have built! Yet give attention to Your servant's prayer that Your eyes may be open toward this temple night and day. When Your people Israel have been defeated by an enemy; when famine or plague[3] comes to the land; and whatever disaster or disease may come, when a prayer or plea[4] is made by any of Your people Israel, then hear their prayer and their plea, and forgive Your people, who have sinned against You."

Explanatory Notes

[1]Solomon was 20 years old when he became king. [2]Are not large enough to hold You. [3]Trouble. [4]Humble request.

The glory of the LORD filled the temple.

For Reflection

1. How did Solomon evidence his faith in the request he made of God?
2. The glory of the Lord filled the temple Solomon had made. In what way does the glory of the Lord fill our churches when God's people gather there for worship?
3. Why does God, who, in Solomon's words, can't be contained by the highest heaven, listen to our prayers?

Words to Remember

If any of you lacks wisdom, he should ask God, ... and it will be given to him. *James 1:5*

The Prophet Elijah

1 Kings 16–17

Ahab became king of Israel. Ahab began to serve Baal[1] and did more to provoke the God of Israel to anger than did all the kings of Israel before him. Now Elijah the prophet said to Ahab, "As the LORD, the God of Israel, lives, there will be neither dew nor rain in the next few years except at My word."

Then the word of the LORD came to Elijah: "Hide in the Kerith Ravine. You will drink from the brook, and I have ordered the ravens to feed you there." So he did what the LORD had told him. The ravens brought him bread and meat in the morning and in the evening, and he drank from the brook.

Some time later the brook dried up because there had been no rain in the land. Then the word of the LORD came to him: "Go at once to Zarephath. I have commanded a widow in that place to supply you with food."

So he went to Zarephath. When he came to the town gate, a widow was there gathering sticks. He called to her and asked, "Would you bring me a little water so I may have a drink?" As she was going to get it, he called, "And bring me, please, a piece of bread."

She replied, "I don't have any bread—only a handful of flour in a jar and a little oil in a jug to make a meal for myself and my son, that we may eat it—and die."

Elijah said to her, "Don't be afraid. For this is what the LORD, the God of Israel, says: 'The jar of flour will not be used up and the jug of oil will not run dry until the day the LORD gives rain on the land.'" So there was food every day for Elijah and for the woman and her family. For the jar of flour was not used up and the jug of oil did not run dry, in keeping with the word of the Lord.

Some time later the son of the woman became ill. He grew worse and worse, and finally stopped breathing. "Give me your son," Elijah replied. Then he cried out to the LORD. The LORD heard Elijah's cry, and the boy's life returned to him, and he lived.

Explanatory Notes
[1] A false god, an idol.

Ravens brought him bread and meat ... and he drank from the brook.

For Reflection
1. In what ways did God provide for His servant Elijah?
2. How did God show His power over death? What does Jesus' victory over death mean for us as the children of God?
3. How does God help you in times of need or trouble?

Words to Remember

The eyes of the LORD are on those who fear Him, on those whose hope is in His unfailing love, to deliver them from death and keep them alive in famine. *Psalm 33:18–19*

Elijah and the Prophets of Baal

1 Kings 18

Elijah went before the people and said, "How long will you waver between two opinions? If the LORD is God, follow Him; but if Baal is God, follow him." But the people said nothing. Then Elijah said to them, "Get two bulls for us. Let the prophets of Baal choose one for themselves, and put it on the wood but not set fire to it. I will prepare the other bull and put it on the wood but not set fire to it. Then you call on the name of your god, and I will call on the name of the LORD. The god who answers by fire—He is God."

Then all the people said, "What you say is good."

Elijah said to the prophets of Baal, "Choose one of these bulls and prepare it." Then they called on the name of Baal from morning till noon. "O Baal, answer us!" they shouted. But there was no response; no one answered.

Then Elijah said to all the people, "Come here to me." They came to him, and he repaired the altar of the LORD, which was in ruins. He dug a trench around the altar, arranged the wood, and laid the bull on the wood. Then he said to them, "Fill four large jars with water and pour it on the offering and on the wood."

"Do it again," he said, and they did it again. "Do it a third time," he ordered, and they did it the third time. The water ran down around the altar and even filled the trench. Elijah stepped forward and prayed: "O LORD, God of Abraham, Isaac and Israel, let it be known today that You are God in Israel and that I am Your servant. Answer me, O LORD, answer me."

Then the fire of the LORD fell and burned up the sacrifice, the wood, the stones and the soil, and also licked up the water in the trench. When all the people saw this, they fell prostrate and cried, "The LORD—He is God! The LORD—He is God!"

Then Elijah commanded them, "Seize the prophets of Baal." They seized them, and Elijah had them brought down to the Kishon Valley and slaughtered there.

The fire of the LORD fell and burned up the sacrifice, the wood, the stones, and the soil.

For Reflection
1. What false god did the people worship in Elijah's day? In what false gods do we sometimes place our trust?
2. How did God show His power to the people of Elijah's day? How did Jesus show His power over sin and evil?
3. Elijah alone defended the true God. When are we called to take an unpopular stand because of our faith in Jesus?

Words to Remember
Worship the Lord your God, and serve Him only. *Matthew 4:10*

Naboth's Vineyard

1 Kings 21

There was a vineyard belonging to Naboth, close to the palace of Ahab king of Samaria. Ahab said to Naboth, "Let me have your vineyard, since it is close to my palace. In exchange I will give you a better vineyard or, if you prefer, I will pay you whatever it is worth."

But Naboth replied, "The LORD forbid that I should give you the inheritance of my fathers."

So Ahab went home, sullen and angry. He lay on his bed sulking and refused to eat. His wife Jezebel came in and said, "Get up and eat! Cheer up. I'll get you the vineyard of Naboth."

So she wrote letters in Ahab's name, placed his seal on them, and sent them to the elders and nobles who lived in Naboth's city with him. In those letters she wrote: "Proclaim a day of fasting[1] and seat Naboth in a prominent place among the people.[2] Seat two scoundrels opposite him and have them testify that he has cursed both God and the king. Then take him out and stone him to death."[3] So they did as Jezebel directed.

As soon as Jezebel heard that Naboth had been stoned to death, she said to Ahab, "Get up and take possession of the vineyard of Naboth. He is dead."

Then the word of the LORD came to Elijah: "Go down to meet Ahab king of Israel. He is now in Naboth's vineyard, where he has gone to take possession of it. Say to him, 'This is what the LORD says: Have you not murdered a man and seized his property? In the place where dogs licked up Naboth's blood, dogs will lick up your blood!' Dogs will devour[4] Jezebel by the wall of Jezreel. Dogs will eat those belonging to Ahab who die in the city, and the birds of the air will feed on those who die in the country."

And all of it happened as the word of the LORD had declared.

Explanatory Notes

[1]As a sign that something terrible had happened. [2]Naboth could then be quickly and openly accused. [3]Cursing or blaspheming was punishable by death. [4]Eat.

Ahab went home, sullen and angry.

For Reflection

1. Ahab coveted the property of Naboth. Tell how coveting led Ahab and Jezebel to commit other sins.
2. What can we learn from this story about the consequences of sin?
3. In the New Testament, another innocent man was put to death so that an undeserved inheritance might be claimed by many—including you and me. Explain.

Words to Remember

For God did not send His Son into the world to condemn the world, but to save the world through Him. *John 3:17*

95

Elisha Sees Elijah Ascend[1]

2 Kings 2

When the LORD was about to take Elijah up to heaven in a whirlwind, Elijah and Elisha were on their way from Gilgal. Elijah took his cloak, rolled it up and struck the water with it. The water divided to the right and to the left, and the two of them crossed over on dry ground.

When they had crossed, Elijah said to Elisha, "Tell me, what can I do for you before I am taken from you?"

"Let me inherit a double portion of your spirit,"[2] Elisha replied.

"You have asked a difficult thing," Elijah said, "yet if you see me when I am taken from you, it will be yours—otherwise not."

As they were walking along and talking together, suddenly a chariot of fire and horses of fire appeared, and Elijah went up to heaven in a whirlwind. Elisha saw this and cried out, "My father! My father! The chariots and horsemen of Israel!" And Elisha saw him no more.

He picked up the cloak that had fallen from Elijah and went back and stood on the bank of the Jordan. Then he took the cloak that had fallen from him and struck the water with it. "Where now is the LORD, the God of Elijah?" he asked. When he struck the water, it divided to the right and to the left, and he crossed over. The company of prophets from Jericho who were watching said, "The spirit of Elijah is resting on Elisha."

Explanatory Notes

[1]Going up into heaven. [2]Elisha desired the power of Elijah to do the Lord's work in the best possible way.

Elisha saw this and cried out, "My father! My father!"

For Reflection
1. What did Elisha ask of Elijah?
2. How did Elijah go to heaven?
3. How does God's Spirit come to—and work in—the lives of God's people today?

Words to Remember
I have fought the good fight, I have finished the race, I have kept the faith. Now there is in store for me the crown of righteousness. *2 Timothy 4:7–8*

Naaman and Elisha

2 Kings 5

Now Naaman was commander of the army of the king of Aram. He was a great man, but he had leprosy. Now bands from Aram had taken captive a young girl from Israel, and she served Naaman's wife. She said to her mistress, "If only my master would see the prophet who is in Samaria! He would cure him of his leprosy."

So Naaman left, taking with him ten talents of silver, six thousand shekels of gold, and ten sets of clothing. Naaman went with his horses and chariots and stopped at the door of Elisha's house.

Elisha sent a messenger to say to him, "Go, wash yourself seven times in the Jordan, and you will be cleansed."[1] But Naaman went away angry and said, "Are not the rivers of Damascus better than any of the waters of Israel?" So he turned and went off in a rage. Naaman's servants went to him and said, "My father, if the prophet had told you to do some great thing, would you not have done it?" So he went down and dipped himself in the Jordan seven times, and he became clean.

Then Naaman and all his attendants went back to the man of God and said, "Now I know that there is no God in all the world except in Israel. Please accept now a gift from your servant." The prophet answered, "As surely as the Lord lives, whom I serve, I will not accept a thing." But even though Naaman urged him, Elisha refused.

After Naaman had traveled some distance, Gehazi, the servant of Elisha, hurried after Naaman and said, "My master sent me to say, 'Two young men from the company of the prophets have just come to me. Please give them a talent of silver and two sets of clothing.'" "By all means, take two talents," said Naaman. Gehazi took the things and put them away in the house. Then he went in and stood before his master Elisha.

"Where have you been, Gehazi?" Elisha asked. "Your servant didn't go anywhere," Gehazi answered. But Elisha said to him, "Is this the time to take money, or to accept clothes? Naaman's leprosy will cling to you and to your descendants forever." Then Gehazi went from Elisha's presence and he was leprous, as white as snow.

Explanatory Notes
[1]Healed.

She said to her mistress, "If only my master would see the prophet."

For Reflection

1. How did the young girl in this story share God's love with those who held her captive?
2. How was Naaman cured of his leprosy?
3. How are we "cured" of the disease of sin?

Words to Remember

He saved us through the washing of rebirth and renewal by the Holy Spirit, whom He poured out on us generously through Jesus Christ our Savior. *Titus 3:5–6*

God Sends Jonah

Jonah 1–3

The word of the LORD came to Jonah son of Amittai: "Go to the great city of Nineveh and preach against it, because its wickedness has come up before Me." But Jonah ran away from the LORD and headed for Tarshish.[1] He went down to Joppa, where he found a ship bound for that port. After paying the fare, he went aboard and sailed for Tarshish to flee from the LORD.

Then the LORD sent a great wind on the sea, and such a violent storm arose that the ship threatened to break up. The sea was getting rougher and rougher. So the sailors asked Jonah, "What should we do to you to make the sea calm down for us?"

"Pick me up and throw me into the sea," he replied, "and it will become calm. I know that it is my fault that this great storm has come upon you." Then they took Jonah and threw him overboard, and the raging sea grew calm. But the LORD provided a great fish to swallow Jonah, and Jonah was inside the fish three days and three nights.

From inside the fish Jonah prayed to the LORD his God. He said: "In my distress I called to the LORD, and He answered me. From the depths of the grave I called for help, and You listened to my cry." And the LORD commanded the fish, and it vomited Jonah onto dry land.

Then the word of the LORD came to Jonah a second time: "Go to the great city of Nineveh and proclaim to it the message I give you." Jonah obeyed the word of the LORD and went to Nineveh. Now Nineveh was a very important city—a visit required three days.

On the first day, Jonah started into the city. He proclaimed: "Forty more days and Nineveh will be overturned." The Ninevites believed God. They declared a fast,[2] and all of them, from the greatest to the least, put on sackcloth.

When God saw what they did and how they turned from their evil ways, He had compassion and did not bring upon them the destruction He had threatened.

Explanatory Notes
[1]Perhaps an ancient city in modern-day Spain. [2]A day of repentance and sorrow; no eating and drinking were permitted.

"In my distress I called to the LORD."

For Reflection
1. Why did Jonah run away from the Lord?
2. How did God show His kindness to Jonah in spite of Jonah's disobedience?
3. Jesus came to earth to die for our sins, earning our salvation for us. How does Jesus' death and resurrection compare to Jonah's experience inside the great fish?

Words to Remember

For as Jonah was three days and three nights in the belly of a huge fish, so the Son of Man will be three days and three nights in the heart of the earth. *Matthew 12:40*

Jeremiah

Jeremiah 37–38

The word of the LORD came to Jeremiah the prophet: "This is what the LORD, the God of Israel, says: Tell the king of Judah, who sent you to inquire of Me, 'Pharaoh's army, which has marched out to support you, will go back to its own land, to Egypt. Then the Babylonians will return and attack this city; they will capture it and burn it down.'"

Then the officials said to the king, "This man should be put to death. He is discouraging the soldiers who are left in this city, as well as all the people, by the things he is saying to them. This man is not seeking the good of these people but their ruin."

"He is in your hands," King Zedekiah answered. "The king can do nothing to oppose you." So they took Jeremiah and put him into the cistern[1] which was in the courtyard of the guard. They lowered Jeremiah by ropes into the cistern; it had no water in it, only mud, and Jeremiah sank down into the mud.

But Ebed-Melech, a Cushite,[2] an official in the royal palace, heard that they had put Jeremiah into the cistern. While the king was sitting in the Benjamin Gate, Ebed-Melech went out of the palace and said to him, "My lord the king, these men have acted wickedly in all they have done to Jeremiah the prophet. They have thrown him into a cistern, where he will starve to death when there is no longer any bread in the city." Then the king commanded Ebed-Melech the Cushite, "Take thirty men from here with you and lift Jeremiah the prophet out of the cistern before he dies." So Ebed-Melech took the men with him and went to a room under the treasury in the palace. He took some old rags and worn-out clothes from there and let them down with ropes to Jeremiah in the cistern.

Ebed-Melech the Cushite said to Jeremiah, "Put these old rags and worn-out clothes under your arms to pad the ropes." Jeremiah did so, and they pulled him up with the ropes and lifted him out of the cistern.

Explanatory Notes

[1]A hole in the ground for storing water. [2]One from ancient Ethiopia; his name means "king's servant."

"Lift Jeremiah the prophet out of the cistern."

For Reflection
1. Why was Jeremiah thrown in the cistern?
2. Why did Ebed-Melech want to help Jeremiah?
3. How has Jesus rescued you in your troubles?

Words to Remember

I was overcome by trouble and sorrow. Then I called on the name of the LORD: "O LORD, save me!" *Psalm 116:3–4.*

The Three Men in the Fiery Furnace

Daniel 3

King Nebuchadnezzar made an image[1] of gold, and summoned all the provincial officials to come to the dedication of the image. Then the herald loudly proclaimed, "O people, as soon as you hear the sound of music, you must fall down and worship the image of gold. Whoever does not fall down and worship will immediately be thrown into a blazing furnace." Therefore, as soon as they heard the sound of music, all the people fell down and worshiped the image of gold.

At this time some astrologers came forward and denounced[2] the Jews. They said to King Nebuchadnezzar, "O king, Shadrach, Meshach and Abednego do not worship the image of gold."

Furious with rage, Nebuchadnezzar summoned Shadrach, Meshach and Abednego and said to them, "If you do not worship my image, you will be thrown immediately into a blazing furnace. Then what god will be able to rescue you from my hand?"

Shadrach, Meshach and Abednego replied to the king, "If we are thrown into the blazing furnace, the God we serve is able to save us from it. But even if He does not, we want you to know, O king, that we will not worship the image of gold."

Then Nebuchadnezzar was furious with them. He ordered the furnace heated seven times hotter than usual and commanded some of the strongest soldiers in his army to tie up Shadrach, Meshach and Abednego and throw them into the blazing furnace.

Then King Nebuchadnezzar leaped to his feet in amazement and asked his advisers, "Weren't there three men that we tied up and threw into the fire? Look! I see four men walking around in the fire, unbound and unharmed, and the fourth looks like a son of the gods." Nebuchadnezzar then approached the opening of the blazing furnace and shouted, "Servants of the Most High God, come out!" They did, and not a hair of their heads was singed; their robes were not scorched, and there was no smell of fire on them.

Then Nebuchadnezzar said, "Praise be to the God of Shadrach, Meshach and Abednego, who has sent His angel and rescued His servants who trusted in Him."

Explanatory Notes
[1]Statue. [2]Spoke against.

"The God we serve is able to save us."

For Reflection

1. How did Shadrach, Meshach, and Abednego live out their faith in the one true God?
2. How did God save the three young men who trusted in Him?
3. What temptations do you face to deny your faith in Jesus? In what ways does Jesus rescue you?

Words to Remember

And the God of all grace, who called you to His eternal glory in Christ, after you have suffered a little while, will Himself restore you and make you strong, firm and steadfast. *1 Peter 5:10*

Daniel in the Lions' Den

Daniel 6

King Darius appointed three administrators to rule throughout the kingdom, one of whom was Daniel. Now Daniel so distinguished himself by his exceptional qualities that the king planned to set him over the whole kingdom. At this, the administrators tried to find grounds for charges against Daniel, but they were unable to do so. Finally these men said, "We will never find any basis for charges against this man Daniel unless it has something to do with the law of his God."

So they went as a group to the king and said: "King Darius, the royal administrators, advisers, and governors have all agreed that the king should issue an edict[1] that anyone who prays to any god or man during the next thirty days, except to you, O king, shall be thrown into the lions' den." So King Darius put the decree in writing.

Now when Daniel learned that the decree had been published, he went home to his upstairs room where the windows opened toward Jerusalem. Three times a day he got down on his knees and prayed, just as he had done before.

Then these men went as a group to the king and spoke to him: "Daniel pays no attention to you, O king. He still prays three times a day." When the king heard this, he was greatly distressed; he was determined to rescue Daniel. But the men said to him, "Remember, O king, that no decree or edict that the king issues can be changed."

So they brought Daniel and threw him into the lions' den. The king said to Daniel, "May your God, whom you serve continually, rescue you!"

The king spent the night without eating and he could not sleep. At the first light of dawn, the king got up and hurried to the lions' den. He called, "Daniel, has your God been able to rescue you from the lions?"

Daniel answered, "My God sent His angel, and He shut the mouths of the lions. They have not hurt me."

The king was overjoyed and gave orders to lift Daniel out of the den. At the king's command, the men who had falsely accused Daniel were brought in and thrown into the lions' den. Then King Darius wrote to all the people: "Reverence the God of Daniel. For He is the living God and He endures forever."

Explanatory Notes
[1]A proclamation having the force of law.

"God sent His angel, and He shut the mouths of the lions."

For Reflection

1. Why did the administrators and other leaders work to find fault with Daniel?
2. How did God protect Daniel?
3. Do you think Daniel was afraid? Why need we not be afraid when put in scary situations?

Words to Remember

So do not fear, for I am with you; do not be dismayed, for I am your God. I will strengthen you and help you; I will uphold you with My righteous right hand. *Isaiah 41:10*

A Message for Zechariah

Luke 1

In the time of Herod king of Judea there was a priest named Zechariah, and his wife Elizabeth. Both of them were upright in the sight of God, but they had no children, and they were both well along in years.

Once when Zechariah's division was on duty and he was serving as priest before God, he was chosen by lot to go into the temple of the Lord and burn incense.[1] And when the time for the burning of incense came, all the assembled worshipers were praying outside. Then an angel of the Lord appeared to him, standing at the right side of the altar of incense.

When Zechariah saw him, he was startled and was gripped with fear. But the angel said to him: "Do not be afraid, Zechariah; your prayer has been heard. Your wife Elizabeth will bear you a son, and you are to give him the name John. He will be great in the sight of the Lord and will be filled with the Holy Spirit. And he will go on before the Lord, in the spirit and power of Elijah, to make ready a people prepared for the Lord."[2]

Zechariah asked the angel, "How can I be sure of this?"

The angel answered, "I am Gabriel. I stand in the presence of God, and I have been sent to tell you this good news. And now you will not be able to speak until the day this happens, because you did not believe my words."

Meanwhile, the people were waiting for Zechariah and wondering why he stayed so long in the temple. When he came out, he could not speak to them. He kept making signs to them but remained unable to speak.

Explanatory Notes

[1]Made from the sap of trees; prescribed for offering in Exodus 30:34–36, and having a pleasant fragrance when burned. [2]He was to prepare the people for the coming of the Savior by telling them about Him.

"I have been sent to tell you this good news."

For Reflection

1. Tell how God provided Zechariah with good news. Why was this good news so unusual?

2. What did Gabriel tell Zechariah about John's role and mission in life?

3. What message of good news has the Lord brought to you? How can you "be sure" of it?

Words to Remember

See, I will send My messenger, who will prepare the way before Me. *Malachi 3:1*

The Announcement to Mary

Matthew 1; Luke 1

In the sixth month,[1] God sent the angel Gabriel to Nazareth to a virgin pledged to be married[2] to a man named Joseph, a descendant of David. The virgin's name was Mary. The angel went to her and said, "Greetings, you who are highly favored![3] The Lord is with you."

Mary was greatly troubled at his words and wondered what kind of greeting this might be.

But the angel said to her, "Do not be afraid, Mary, you have found favor with God. You will give birth to a son, and you are to give Him the name Jesus. He will be great and will be called the Son of the Most High. He will reign over the house of Jacob forever."

"How will this be," Mary asked the angel, "since I am a virgin?"[4]

The angel answered, "The Holy Spirit will come upon you, and the power of the Most High will overshadow you. So the Holy One to be born will be called the Son of God. For nothing is impossible with God."

"I am the Lord's servant," Mary answered. "May it be to me as you have said." Then the angel left her.

An angel of the Lord appeared to Joseph in a dream and said, "Joseph son of David, do not be afraid to take Mary home as your wife, because what is conceived in her is from the Holy Spirit. She will give birth to a son, and you are to give Him the name Jesus, because He will save His people from their sins."

Joseph did what the angel of the Lord had commanded him and took Mary home as his wife.

Explanatory Notes

[1]Six months after he had appeared to Zechariah. [2]Engaged. [3]Honored. [4]A person who has not had sexual intercourse.

"I am the Lord's servant."

For Reflection

1. What was Gabriel's message to Mary?
2. The angel of the Lord appeared to Joseph in a dream and told him to name Mary's baby Jesus (Matthew 1). What does the name Jesus mean?
3. One of the names given to Jesus is *Immanuel*, which means "God with us." How is Jesus "God with us"?

Words to Remember

The virgin will be with child and will give birth to a son, and will call Him Immanuel. *Isaiah 7:14*

The Birth of John the Baptist

Luke 1

Elizabeth gave birth to a son. Her neighbors and relatives heard that the Lord had shown her great mercy, and they shared her joy.

On the eighth day they came to circumcise[1] the child, and they were going to name him after his father Zechariah, but his mother spoke up and said, "No! He is to be called John."

They said to her, "There is no one among your relatives who has that name." Then they made signs to his father, to find out what he would like to name the child.

He asked for a writing tablet,[2] and to everyone's astonishment he wrote, "His name is John." Immediately his mouth was opened and his tongue was loosed,[3] and he began to speak, praising God.

The neighbors were all filled with awe. Everyone who heard this wondered about it, asking, "What then is this child going to be?" For the Lord's hand was with him.

His father Zechariah was filled with the Holy Spirit and prophesied:[4] "Praise be to the Lord, the God of Israel, because He has come and has redeemed His people.[5] And you, my child, will be called a prophet of the Most High; for you will go on before the Lord[6] to prepare the way for Him, to give His people the knowledge of salvation[7] through the forgiveness of their sins."

And the child grew and became strong in spirit; and he lived in the desert until he appeared publicly to Israel.

Explanatory Notes

[1]According to God's command; see Genesis 17:10–14. [2]Small board covered with wax, used with a stylus stick for writing. [3]He was able to talk. [4]Foretold what would happen. [5]Through Jesus, the Savior. [6]Before Jesus. [7]Tell them how to be saved.

He wrote, "His name is John."

For Reflection

1. Why were people surprised that Zechariah and Elizabeth named their baby John?

2. When did Zechariah regain his speech? What did Zechariah say after he became able to talk?

3. How has God redeemed His people, including you and me?

Words to Remember

The word of the LORD is right. *Psalm 33:4*

113

The Birth of Jesus[1]

Luke 2

In those days Caesar Augustus[2] issued a decree[3] that a census[4] should be taken of the entire Roman world. (This was the first census that took place while Quirinius was governor of Syria.) And everyone went to his own town[5] to register.

So Joseph also went up from the town of Nazareth in Galilee to Judea, to Bethlehem the town of David, because he belonged to the house and line[6] of David. He went there to register with Mary, who was pledged[7] to be married to him and was expecting a child.

While they were there, the time came for the baby to be born, and she gave birth to her firstborn, a son. She wrapped Him in cloths and placed Him in a manger,[8] because there was no room for them in the inn.

Explanatory Notes

[1]The coming of the Savior had been foretold thousands of years before His birth; see Genesis 3:15. Prophets in the Old Testament had prophesied the time of His coming and had said that His mother would be a virgin. One of them had even foretold that He would be born in the town of Bethlehem. [2]Great Roman emperor. Judea, Samaria, and Galilee were among many lands under the control of his empire. [3]A law. [4]Registration. [5]The town where his ancestors were from. [6]Family. [7]Engaged. [8]Feeding trough, or box, for animals.

She wrapped Him in cloths and placed Him in a manger.

For Reflection

1. How did it happen that God's Son was born in Bethlehem when Mary and Joseph lived in Nazareth in Galilee?
2. Jesus' first bed was a manger. What does that tell us about God's Son?
3. Why does this simple story give Christians so much reason to rejoice?

Words to Remember

To us a child is born, to us a son is given. *Isaiah 9:6*

Angels Announce the Savior's Birth

Luke 2

And there were shepherds living out in the fields nearby, keeping watch over their flocks at night. An angel of the Lord appeared to them, and the glory of the Lord shone around them, and they were terrified.

But the angel said to them, "Do not be afraid. I bring you good news of great joy that will be for all the people. Today in the town of David a Savior has been born to you; He is Christ[1] the Lord.[2] This will be a sign to you: You will find a baby wrapped in cloths and lying in a manger."

Suddenly a great company of the heavenly host[3] appeared with the angel, praising God and saying, "Glory to God in the highest, and on earth peace to men on whom His favor rests."

When the angels had left them and gone into heaven, the shepherds said to one another, "Let's go to Bethlehem and see this thing that has happened, which the Lord has told us about." So they hurried off and found Mary and Joseph, and the baby, who was lying in the manger.

When they had seen Him, they spread the word[4] concerning what had been told them about this child, and all who heard it were amazed at what the shepherds said to them.

But Mary treasured up all these things and pondered[5] them in her heart.

Explanatory Notes

[1]The Anointed, the Messiah. [2]God Himself, Yahweh. [3]A great number of angels. [4]Told others whom they met on the way. [5]Thought about.

The glory of the Lord shone around them.

For Reflection

1. According to the message of the angels, for whom had the Savior come?
2. The angels announced to the shepherds the good news. How did the shepherds respond?
3. What is your reaction to the news of Jesus' birth? Why?

Words to Remember

For God so loved the world that He gave His one and only Son, that whoever believes in Him shall not perish but have eternal life. *John 3:16*

The Presentation of Jesus

Luke 2

On the eighth day, when it was time to circumcise[1] Him, He was named Jesus,[2] the name the angel had given Him before He had been conceived.

When the time of their purification[3] according to the Law of Moses had been completed, Joseph and Mary took Him to Jerusalem to present Him to the Lord,[4] and to offer a sacrifice.[5]

Now there was a man in Jerusalem called Simeon, who was righteous and devout.[6] He was waiting for the consolation[7] of Israel, and the Holy Spirit was upon him. It had been revealed[8] to him by the Holy Spirit that he would not die before he had seen the Lord's Christ. Moved by the Spirit, he went into the temple courts. When the parents brought in the child Jesus, Simeon took Him in his arms and praised God, saying: "Sovereign Lord, as You have promised, You now dismiss Your servant in peace.[9] For my eyes have seen Your salvation, which You have prepared in the sight of all people, a light for revelation to the Gentiles[10] and for glory to Your people Israel."

The child's father and mother marveled at what was said about Him.

There was also a prophetess, Anna. She was very old and was a widow. She never left the temple but worshiped night and day, fasting and praying. Coming up to them at that very moment, she gave thanks to God and spoke about the child to all who were looking forward to the redemption of Jerusalem.

Explanatory Notes

[1]The Law of Moses ordered all boy babies to be circumcised on the eighth day after birth; see Leviticus 12:1–3. [2]Meaning Savior. [3]Lasting forty days after a male child was born; see Leviticus 12:2–4. [4]Commanded in Leviticus 12:2–4. [5]Consisting of a pair of turtle doves or two young pigeons; see Leviticus 12:6, 8. [6]God-fearing. [7]The promised Savior. [8]Told. [9]Die happy. [10]Those who are not Jewish.

Simeon took Him in his arms and praised God.

For Reflection

1. For what purpose did Mary and Joseph bring Jesus to the temple?
2. Why did Simeon and Anna bless and thank the Lord?
3. Simeon said he could die "in peace." Because of Jesus, why can we have peace even at the point of death?

Words to Remember

When the time had fully come, God sent His Son, born of a woman, born under law, to redeem those under the law. *Galatians 4:4*

The Magi from the East

Matthew 2

After Jesus was born in Bethlehem, Magi[1] from the east[2] came to Jerusalem and asked, "Where is the One who has been born king of the Jews? We saw His star in the east and have come to worship Him."

When King Herod heard this he was disturbed,[3] and all Jerusalem with him. When he had called together all the people's chief priests and teachers of the law, he asked them where the Christ was to be born. "In Bethlehem in Judea," they replied, "for this is what the prophet has written: 'But you, Bethlehem, in the land of Judah, are by no means least among the rulers of Judah; for out of you will come a ruler who will be the shepherd of My people Israel.'"[4]

Then Herod called the Magi secretly and found out from them the exact time the star had appeared. He sent them to Bethlehem and said, "Go and make a careful search for the child. As soon as you find Him, report to me, so that I too may go and worship Him."

After they had heard the king, they went on their way, and the star they had seen in the east went ahead of them until it stopped over the place where the child was. When they saw the star, they were overjoyed. On coming to the house, they saw the child with His mother Mary, and they bowed down and worshiped Him. Then they opened their treasures and presented Him with gifts of gold and of incense and of myrrh.[5]

And having been warned in a dream not to go back to Herod, they returned to their country by another route.

Explanatory Notes

[1]Learned, or wise, men. Simeon's words that Jesus should be "a light for revelation to the Gentiles" were already being fulfilled. [2]East of Palestine, perhaps Persia or southern Arabia. [3]Worried. [4]Micah 5:2. [5]A gift fit for a king, and later applied to Jesus' body after He was crucified.

Coming to the house, they saw the child.

For Reflection

1. How did King Herod learn the birthplace of the Savior?
2. What does the coming of the Magi signify for persons who are not of Jewish descent?
3. Why were the Magi "overjoyed" when they saw the star? Do we have the same reason? Why or why not?

Words to Remember

Nations will come to Your light, and kings to the brightness of Your dawn. *Isaiah 60:3*

The Escape to Egypt

Matthew 2

When they[1] had gone, an angel of the Lord appeared to Joseph in a dream. "Get up," he said, "take the child and His mother and escape to Egypt. Stay there until I tell you, for Herod is going to search for the child to kill Him."[2]

So he got up, took the child and His mother during the night and left for Egypt, where he stayed until the death of Herod. And so was fulfilled what the Lord had said through the prophet: "Out of Egypt I called My Son."[3]

When Herod realized that he had been outwitted by the Magi, he was furious, and he gave orders to kill all the boys in Bethlehem and its vicinity who were two years old and under, in accordance with the time he had learned from the Magi.

After Herod died, an angel of the Lord appeared in a dream to Joseph in Egypt and said, "Get up, take the child and His mother and go to the land of Israel, for those who were trying to take the child's life are dead."

So he got up, took the child and His mother and went to the land of Israel, and lived in a town called Nazareth. So was fulfilled what was said through the prophets: "He will be called a Nazarene."

Explanatory Notes

[1]The Wise Men. [2]Jesus had come into this sinful world to redeem all men, for all men are sinners. When He was born in Bethlehem, some people came to greet and honor Him; but some showed themselves as His bitter enemies and even wanted to kill Him. [3]See Hosea 11:1.

He got up, took the Child and His mother during the night and left.

For Reflection

1. How did God take care of His Son?
2. Why was Herod determined to find and kill Jesus? How did God guide the Magi to "outwit" Herod?
3. By faith, we too are the children of God. How does God take care of us?

Words to Remember

How great is the love the Father has lavished on us, that we should be called children of God! And that is what we are! The reason the world does not know us is that it did not know Him. *1 John 3:1*

The Boy Jesus at the Temple[1]

Luke 2

Every year His parents went to Jerusalem for the Feast of the Passover.[2] When He was twelve years old, they went up to the Feast, according to the custom. After the Feast was over, while His parents were returning home, the boy Jesus stayed behind in Jerusalem, but they were unaware of it. Thinking He was in their company,[3] they traveled on for a day. Then they began looking for Him among their relatives and friends. When they did not find Him, they went back to Jerusalem to look for Him.

After three days they found Him in the temple courts, sitting among the teachers, listening to them and asking them questions. Everyone who heard Him was amazed at His understanding and His answers. When His parents saw Him, they were astonished.[4] His mother said to Him, "Son, why have You treated us like this? Your father and I have been anxiously searching for You."

"Why were you searching for Me?" He asked. "Didn't you know I had to be in My Father's house?"

But they did not understand what He was saying to them.

Then He went down to Nazareth with them and was obedient to them. But His mother treasured all these things in her heart.

And Jesus grew in wisdom and stature,[5] and in favor with[6] God and men.

Explanatory Notes

[1]This is the only story in the Bible which tells us something about the Savior while He was a boy of school age in Nazareth. [2]One of three great Jewish festivals, also known as the Feast of Unleavened Bread. [3]People who had traveled with them. [4]Did not know what to think. [5]Age. [6]Was deeply loved by.

They found Him in the temple courts, sitting among the teachers.

For Reflection

1. Why did Jesus' parents go to Jerusalem every year?
2. What do you think Jesus meant when He asked, "Didn't you know I had to be in My Father's house?"
3. Where can we find Jesus today? What does He say to us?

Words to Remember

In Christ are hidden all the treasures of wisdom and knowledge. *Colossians 2:3*

The Baptism of Jesus

Matthew 3; Mark 1

In those days John the Baptist[1] came, preaching in the Desert[2] of Judea and went into all the country around the Jordan, saying, "Repent,[3] for the kingdom of heaven is near." This is he who was spoken of through the prophet Isaiah: "A voice of one calling in the desert, 'Prepare the way for the Lord, make straight paths for him.'"

John's clothes were made of camel's hair, and he had a leather belt around his waist. His food was locusts[4] and wild honey. People went out to him from Jerusalem and all Judea and the whole region of the Jordan. Confessing their sins, they were baptized by him in the Jordan River.

When all the people were being baptized, then Jesus came from Galilee to the Jordan to be baptized. But John tried to deter[5] Him, saying, "I need to be baptized by You, and do You come to me?"

Jesus replied, "Let it be so now; it is proper for us to do this to fulfill all righteousness."[6] Then John consented.

As Jesus was coming up out of the water, He saw heaven being torn open and the Spirit descending[7] on Him like a dove.[8] And a voice[9] came from heaven: "You are My Son, whom I love; with You I am well pleased."

Explanatory Notes

[1]John the Baptist was Jesus' forerunner, who prepared His way. Jesus was about 30 years old and ready to make Himself known as the Savior. [2]The region along the Jordan and near the Dead Sea. [3]Turn from your sins. [4]Grasshoppers. [5]Stop Him. [6]Do God's will. [7]Coming down. [8]Representing the gentleness, peace, and purity of the Holy Spirit. [9]The voice of God the Father.

"You are My Son, whom I love."

For Reflection
1. Describe the appearance and work of John.
2. The three Persons of the Trinity can be clearly identified at Jesus' Baptism. Explain.
3. Jesus came to "fulfill all righteousness," or do God's will. This includes His death. Why did He have to die? (See verse in "Words to Remember.")

Words to Remember

God made Him who had no sin to be sin for us, so that in Him we might become the righteousness of God. *2 Corinthians 5:21*

127

The Temptation of Jesus[1]

Matthew 4

Then Jesus was led by the Spirit into the desert to be tempted[2] by the devil. After fasting[3] forty days and forty nights, He was hungry. The tempter came to Him and said, "If You are the Son of God, tell these stones to become bread."

Jesus answered, "It is written: 'Man does not live on bread alone, but on every word that comes from the mouth of God.'"

Then the devil took Him to the holy city[4] and had Him stand on the highest point of the temple. "If You are the Son of God," he said, "throw yourself down. For it is written: 'He will command His angels concerning you, and they will lift you up in their hands, so that you will not strike your foot against a stone.'"

Jesus answered him, "It is also written: 'Do not put the Lord your God to the test.'"

Again, the devil took Him to a very high mountain and showed Him all the kingdoms of the world and their splendor. "All this I will give You," he said, "if You will bow down and worship me."[5]

Jesus said to him, "Away from Me, Satan! For it is written: 'Worship the Lord your God, and serve Him only.'"

Then the devil left Him, and angels came and attended Him.

Explanatory Notes

[1]Jesus showed Himself to be faithful when faced with temptation, and displayed His qualifications to be Savior. Because He is perfect, He overcame sin and temptation for us, and also became a model for all believers when they are tempted. [2]Tried, tested. [3]He had not eaten. [4]Jerusalem. [5]Honor, pray to.

"Worship the Lord your God, and serve Him only."

For Reflection
1. What did Jesus use in response to the devil's temptation?
2. Jesus resisted the devil's power. What does this show us about Jesus?
3. What does Jesus' victory over temptation mean for us in our daily Christian lives?

Words to Remember

We have one who has been tempted in every way, just as we are—yet was without sin. *Hebrews 4:15*

129

Jesus Helps Peter Catch Fish

Luke 5

One day as Jesus was standing by the Lake of Gennesaret, with the people crowding around Him and listening to the Word of God, He saw at the water's edge two boats, left there by the fishermen, who were washing their nets. He got into one of the boats, the one belonging to Simon, and asked him to put out a little from shore. Then He sat down and taught the people from the boat.[1]

When He had finished speaking, He said to Simon, "Put[2] out into deep water, and let down the nets for a catch."

Simon answered, "Master, we've worked hard all night and haven't caught anything. But because You say so, I will let down the nets." When they had done so, they caught such a large number of fish that their nets began to break. So they signaled their partners in the other boat to come and help them, and they came and filled both boats so full that they began to sink.

When Simon Peter saw this, he fell at Jesus' knees and said, "Go away from me, Lord; I am a sinful man!" For he and all his companions were astonished at the catch of fish they had taken, and so were James and John, Simon's partners.

Then Jesus said to Simon, "Don't be afraid; from now on you will catch men."

So they pulled their boats up on shore, left everything and followed Him.

Explanatory Notes

[1]Wherever Jesus was seen, people gathered around Him in large numbers to hear Him speak. The boat allowed Him to be away from the crowd, but still close enough to be heard. [2]Row.

They caught ... a large number of fish.

For Reflection

1. How did Jesus take care of the needs of the people? How does Jesus provide for our needs?
2. How did Simon Peter react to Jesus after the miracle of the large catch of fish?
3. What new direction in life did Jesus give to Simon Peter? What new direction does Jesus bring to our lives?

Words to Remember

For you have been born again, not of perishable seed, but of imperishable, through the living and enduring word of God. *1 Peter 1:23*

131

Jesus Changes Water to Wine

John 2

On the third day a wedding took place at Cana in Galilee. Jesus' mother was there, and Jesus and His disciples had also been invited to the wedding.

When the wine was gone, Jesus' mother said to Him, "They have no more wine."

"Dear woman, why do you involve Me?" Jesus replied. "My time has not yet come."

His mother said to the servants, "Do whatever He tells you."

Nearby stood six stone water jars, the kind used by the Jews for ceremonial washing,[1] each holding from twenty to thirty gallons. Jesus said to the servants, "Fill the jars with water." So they filled them to the brim.

Then He told them, "Now draw some out and take it to the master of the banquet." They did so, and the master of the banquet tasted the water that had been turned into wine. He did not realize where it had come from, though the servants who had drawn the water knew. Then he called the bridegroom aside and said, "Everyone brings out the choice wine first and then the cheaper wine after the guests have had too much to drink; but you have saved the best till now."

This, the first of His miraculous signs,[2] Jesus performed at Cana in Galilee. He thus revealed His glory, and His disciples put their faith in Him.[3]

Explanatory Notes

[1]Cleansing; see Numbers 31:23–24. [2]Miracles; wonderful events produced by divine power. [3]Their faith was strengthened, and they believed Jesus to be the Son of God.

"Fill the jars with water."

For Reflection
1. Describe Jesus' first miracle.
2. According to the last verse of this account, what happened as a result of Jesus' miracles?
3. What does Jesus' ability to do miracles tell you about Him?

Words to Remember

The Word became flesh and made His dwelling among us. We have seen His glory, the glory of the One and Only, who came from the Father, full of grace and truth. *John 1:14*

Jesus Calms the Storm

Mark 4

One day Jesus said to His disciples, "Let's go over to the other side of the lake." So they got into a boat and set out. As they sailed, He fell asleep.[1]

A furious squall[2] came up, and the waves broke over the boat, so that it was nearly swamped. The disciples went and woke Him, saying, "Lord, save us! We're going to drown!"

He said to His disciples, "Why are you so afraid? Do you still have no faith?" He got up, rebuked[3] the wind and said to the waves, "Quiet! Be still!" Then the wind died down and it was completely calm.

The men were amazed and asked, "What kind of man is this? Even the winds and the waves obey Him!"[4]

Explanatory Notes

[1]Jesus was very tired from a hard day's work and longed for a rest, which shows that He was a true man. But at the same time He was the almighty God Himself, as the disciples were to see. [2]Storm. [3]Commanded it to stop blowing and raging. [4]The disciples could tell that Jesus was more than just a man. By such miracles, Jesus hoped that the disciples would have faith that He was also God.

He got up and rebuked the wind.

For Reflection

1. How, in this account, does Jesus show Himself to be truly human?
2. How, in this account, does Jesus show Himself to be true God?
3. How does Jesus help us during the storms in our life?

Words to Remember

Then Jesus said, ... "All authority in heaven and on earth has been given to Me." *Matthew 28:18*

Jesus Heals a Man Who Was Paralyzed

Mark 2

A few days later, when Jesus again entered Capernaum,[1] the people heard that He had come home. So many gathered that there was no room left, not even outside the door, and He preached the word to them.

Some men came, bringing to Him a paralytic,[2] carried by four of them. Since they could not get him to Jesus because of the crowd, they made an opening in the roof above Jesus and, after digging through it, lowered the mat the paralyzed man was lying on.

When Jesus saw their faith, He said to the paralytic, "Son, your sins are forgiven."

Now some teachers of the law were sitting there, thinking to themselves, "He's blaspheming![3] Who can forgive sins but God alone?"

Immediately Jesus knew what they were thinking in their hearts, and He said to them, "Why are you thinking these things? Which is easier: to say to the paralytic, 'Your sins are forgiven,' or to say, 'Get up, take your mat and walk'? But that you may know that the Son of Man[4] has authority on earth to forgive sins . ..." He said to the paralytic, "I tell you, get up, take your mat and go home."

He got up, took his mat and walked out in full view of them all. This amazed[5] everyone and they praised God, saying, "We have never seen anything like this!"

Explanatory Notes

[1]Capernaum was where Jesus had made His home. [2]A man who could not walk. [3]Mocking God. [4]The incarnate Lord who has divine authority to judge and save. [5]They wondered at Jesus' great power.

"Get up, take your mat and walk."

For Reflection

1. What criticism did Jesus receive when He forgave the paralyzed man his sins?
2. What did Jesus prove to those who criticized Him by healing the paralyzed man?
3. Compare the help Jesus provided the paralyzed man with the help He gives to you.

Words to Remember

He is the true God and eternal life. *1 John 5:20*

A Widow's Son and Jairus' Daughter

Luke 7–8

Soon afterward, Jesus went to a town called Nain, and His disciples and a large crowd went along with Him. As He approached the town gate, a dead person was being carried out—the only son of his mother, and she was a widow.

When the Lord saw her, His heart went out to her and He said, "Don't cry." Then He went up and touched the coffin, and those carrying it stood still. He said, "Young man, I say to you, get up!"

The dead man sat up and began to talk, and Jesus gave him back to his mother.

They were all filled with awe and praised God. "A great prophet has appeared among us," they said. "God has come to help His people."

A man named Jairus, a ruler of the synagogue,[1] came and fell at Jesus' feet, pleading with Him to come to his house because his only daughter, a girl of about twelve, was dying. While Jesus was on His way, someone came from the house of Jairus. "Your daughter is dead," he said. "Don't bother the teacher any more."

Hearing this, Jesus said to Jairus, "Don't be afraid; just believe, and she will be healed."

When Jesus entered the ruler's house and saw the flute players[2] and the noisy[3] crowd, He said, "Go away. The girl is not dead but asleep." But they laughed at Him.

After the crowd had been put outside, He went in and took the girl by the hand, and said to her, "Little girl, I say to you, get up!" Immediately the girl stood up and walked around. He told them to give her something to eat.

News of this spread through all that region.

Explanatory Notes
[1]Officer in a Jewish church. [2]Players of sad music. [3]Wailing and weeping.

He went in and took the girl by the hand.

For Reflection
1. How do both of these events show that God feels our hurt when those we love die?
2. What other event shows Jesus ultimate power over death?
3. What does it mean to you that Jesus brings back to life those who have died?

Words to Remember

Jesus said to her, "I am the resurrection and the life. He who believes in Me will live, even though he dies." *John 11:25*

Jesus Feeds More Than Five Thousand

John 6

Some time after this, Jesus crossed to the far shore of the Sea of Galilee, and a great crowd of people followed Him because they saw the miraculous signs He had performed on the sick.

Then Jesus went up on a mountainside and sat down with His disciples. When Jesus looked up and saw a great crowd coming toward him, He said to Philip, "Where shall we buy bread for these people to eat?" He asked this only to test him, for He already had in mind what He was going to do.

Philip answered him, "Eight months' wages would not buy enough bread for each one to have a bite!"

Andrew said, "Here is a boy with five small barley loaves and two small fish, but how far will they go among so many?"

Jesus said, "Have the people sit down." There was plenty of grass in that place, and the men sat down, about five thousand of them.[1] Jesus then took the loaves, gave thanks, and distributed[2] to those who were seated as much as they wanted. He did the same with the fish.

When they had all had enough to eat, He said to His disciples, "Gather the pieces that are left over. Let nothing be wasted." So they gathered them and filled twelve baskets with the pieces of the five barley loaves left over by those who had eaten.

After the people saw the miraculous sign that Jesus did, they began to say, "Surely this is the Prophet who is to come into the world."[3]

Explanatory Notes

[1]At another time, Jesus fed over four thousand. See Matthew 15:32–39 and Mark 8:1–9. [2]Handed out. [3]The promised Savior and Messiah.

140

"Gather the pieces that are left over."

For Reflection

1. What does the feeding of the multitude teach us about Jesus?
2. What did those who witnessed the miracle conclude about Jesus?
3. In what ways does Jesus provide all your daily needs?

Words to Remember

But seek first His kingdom and His righteousness, and all these things will be given to you as well. *Matthew 6:33*

Jesus Walks on the Water

Matthew 14; Mark 6

Jesus, knowing that the crowd intended to come and make Him king[1] by force, immediately made His disciples get into the boat and go on ahead of Him to Bethsaida, while He dismissed the crowd. After leaving them, He went up on a mountainside to pray.

His disciples went down to the lake, got into a boat, and set off across the lake for Capernaum. By now it was dark, and Jesus had not yet joined them. A strong wind was blowing and the waters grew rough, but the boat was already a considerable distance from land, buffeted[2] by the waves because the wind was against it.

About the fourth watch[3] of the night Jesus went out to them, walking on the lake. He was about to pass by them, when the disciples saw Him walking on the lake. They were terrified. "It's a ghost," they said, and cried out in fear.

But Jesus immediately said to them: "Take courage! It is I. Don't be afraid."

"Lord, if it's You," Peter replied, "tell me to come to You on the water."

"Come," he said. Then Peter got down out of the boat, walked on the water and came toward Jesus. But when he saw the wind, he was afraid and, beginning to sink, cried out, "Lord, save me!"

Immediately Jesus reached out His hand and caught him. "You of little faith," He said, "why did you doubt?" And when they climbed into the boat, the wind died down.

Then those who were in the boat worshiped Him, saying, "Truly You are the Son of God."

Explanatory Notes

[1]After Jesus had fed the five thousand, some of them wanted to make Him their earthly king. Jesus, however, came to be their heavenly King, their Savior from sin. [2]Tossed about. [3]Between three and six o'clock in the morning.

Jesus reached out His hand and caught him.

For Reflection
1. Why do you suppose the people wanted Jesus to be their earthly king?
2. In this account Peter shows himself as a man of faith and a man of doubt. Explain.
3. Like Peter, we all have times when we doubt. How did Jesus help Peter when he doubted? How will Jesus help us?

Words to Remember
Don't be afraid; just believe. *Mark 5:36*

The Faith of a Canaanite Woman[1]

Matthew 15

Leaving that place, Jesus withdrew to the region of Tyre and Sidon. A Canaanite woman, who was Greek, from that vicinity came to Him, crying out, "Lord, Son of David, have mercy on me! My daughter is suffering terribly from demon-possession."

Jesus did not answer a word. So His disciples came to Him and urged Him, "Send her away, for she keeps crying out after us."

He answered, "I was sent only to the lost sheep of Israel."

The woman came and knelt before Him. "Lord, help me!" she said.

He replied, "It is not right to take the children's bread and toss it to their dogs."

"Yes, Lord," she said, "but even the dogs eat the crumbs that fall from their masters' table."

Then Jesus answered, "Woman, you have great faith! Your request is granted." And her daughter was healed from that very hour.

Explanatory Notes

[1]While Jesus was on earth among the people, He was greatly surprised only a few times, once because of men's unbelief (Mark 6:6) and twice at the remarkable faith which certain persons displayed. The first of these was the centurion of Capernaum, the second the woman of Canaan.

"Lord, help me!" she said.

For Reflection
1. Why did Jesus' disciples want Him to send the Canaanite woman away?
2. How did the prayer of the woman to Jesus indicate her great faith?
3. What can we learn from the story of the Caananite woman about prayers offered on behalf of the welfare of others?

Words to Remember

Therefore I tell you, whatever you ask for in prayer, believe that you have received it, and it will be yours. *Mark 11:24*

145

The Ten Lepers

Luke 17

Now on His way to Jerusalem, Jesus traveled along the border between Samaria[1] and Galilee. As He was going into a village, ten men who had leprosy[2] met Him. They stood at a distance and called out in a loud voice, "Jesus, Master, have pity on us!"

When He saw them, He said, "Go, show yourselves to the priests."[3] And as they went, they were cleansed. One of them, when he saw he was healed, came back, praising God in a loud voice. He threw himself at Jesus' feet and thanked Him—and he was a Samaritan.

Jesus asked, "Were not all ten cleansed? Where are the other nine? Was no one found to return and give praise to God except this foreigner?"

Then He said to him, "Rise and go; your faith has made you well."

Explanatory Notes

[1]Samaria was a region between Galilee and Judea. Because of various beliefs and practices in their religion, Samaritans were considered outcasts by Jews. [2]Leprosy is a destructive skin disease. [3]Priests examined lepers and declared the individuals cured of the disease (Leviticus 13:2–3).

He threw himself at Jesus' feet and thanked Him.

For Reflection
1. In what ways was life hard for the lepers?
2. What motivated the one leper to return to Jesus? Why do you suppose the other nine lepers did not come back to Jesus?
3. For what blessings can you thank Jesus today?

Words to Remember
Give thanks to the LORD, for He is good; His love endures forever. *Psalm 107:1*

147

Jesus Blesses the Children[1]

Matthew 18–19

At that time the disciples came to Jesus and asked, "Who is the greatest in the kingdom of heaven?"[2]

He called a little child and had him stand among them. And He said: "I tell you the truth, unless you change and become like little children, you will never enter the kingdom of heaven. Therefore, whoever humbles[3] himself like this child is the greatest in the kingdom of heaven. And whoever welcomes a little child like this in My name welcomes Me. But if anyone causes one of these little ones who believe in Me to sin, it would be better for him to have a large millstone hung around his neck and to be drowned in the depths of the sea. See that you do not look down on one of these little ones. For I tell you that their angels in heaven always see the face of My Father in heaven."

Then little children were brought to Jesus for Him to place his hands on them and pray for them. But the disciples rebuked[4] those who brought them.

When Jesus saw this, He was indignant.[5] He said to them, "Let the little children come to Me, and do not hinder them, for the kingdom of God belongs to such as these. I tell you the truth, anyone who will not receive the kingdom of God like a little child will never enter it."

And He took the children in His arms, put His hands on them and blessed them.

Explanatory Notes

[1]Jesus, the Savior, is the Friend in particular of little children. How highly He thinks of them, and how dearly He loves them is shown here. [2]Before this, the disciples had quarreled among themselves. They had debated which of them would be given the highest place in heaven. [3]Lives in simple, trusting dependence on God. [4]Scolded. [5]Rightfully angry.

He took the children in His arms.

For Reflection

1. What did Jesus mean by the saying, "unless you change and become like little children, you will never enter the kingdom of heaven"?
2. Some people have considered children as unimportant or nuisances. But what does Jesus say about the importance of children?
3. How did Jesus show His love for children?

Words to Remember

From the lips of children and infants You have ordained praise. *Psalm 8:2*

The Transfiguration

Matthew 17

After six days Jesus took with Him Peter, James and John the brother of James, and led them up a high mountain by themselves.

There He was transfigured before them. His face shone like the sun, and His clothes became as white as the light.

Two men, Moses and Elijah, appeared in glorious splendor, talking with Jesus. They spoke about His departure, which He was about to bring to fulfillment at Jerusalem. Peter and his companions were very sleepy, but when they became fully awake, they saw His glory and the two men standing with Him. Peter said to Jesus, "Lord, it is good for us to be here. If you wish, I will put up three shelters—one for You, one for Moses and one for Elijah."

While he was still speaking, a bright cloud enveloped them, and a voice from the cloud said, "This is My Son, whom I love; with Him I am well pleased. Listen to Him!" When the disciples heard this, they fell facedown to the ground, terrified. But Jesus came and touched them. "Get up," He said. "Don't be afraid." When they looked up, they saw no one except Jesus.

As they were coming down the mountain, Jesus instructed them, "Don't tell anyone what you have seen, until the Son of Man has been raised from the dead."

"Lord, it is good for us to be here."

For Reflection

1. To be transfigured is to be changed. Describe Jesus' transfiguration.
2. What topic did Jesus discuss with Moses and Elijah?
3. What does it mean to you that Jesus is the Son of God?

Words to Remember

The Word became flesh and made His dwelling among us. We have seen His glory, the glory of the One and Only, who came from the Father, full of grace and truth. *John 1:14*

151

Zacchaeus

Luke 19

Jesus entered Jericho and was passing through. A man was there by the name of Zacchaeus; he was a chief tax collector[1] and was wealthy. He wanted to see who Jesus was, but being a short man he could not, because of the crowd. So he ran ahead and climbed a sycamore-fig tree to see Him, since Jesus was coming that way.

When Jesus reached the spot, He looked up and said to him, "Zacchaeus, come down immediately. I must stay at your house today."

So he came down at once and welcomed Him gladly.

All the people[2] saw this and began to mutter, "He has gone to be the guest of a 'sinner.'"[3]

But Zacchaeus stood up and said to the Lord, "Look, Lord! Here and now I give half of my possessions to the poor, and if I have cheated anybody out of anything, I will pay back four times the amount."

Jesus said to him, "Today salvation[4] has come to this house, because this man, too, is a son of Abraham. For the Son of Man[5] came to seek and to save what was lost."

Explanatory Notes

[1]Tax collectors were hated by most people because many of them were dishonest. [2]The self-righteous, judgmental people, especially the teachers of the Law and Pharisees. [3]Jesus very often showed Himself as the Friend of sinners, joyfully accepting them as people of God if they were truly sorry for what they had done. The scribes and Pharisees objected to this mercy of Jesus. [4]Great blessing through the forgiveness of sins. [5]Jesus.

"Zacchaeus, come down immediately."

For Reflection
1. What do we know about Zacchaeus?
2. How did Zacchaeus show that he had become a follower of Jesus?
3. How do you know that Jesus came to earth to save you?

Words to Remember
Christ Jesus came into the world to save sinners. *1 Timothy 1:15*

153

The Lost Sheep and the Lost Coin[1]

Luke 15

Now the tax collectors and "sinners" were all gathering around to hear Him. But the Pharisees and the teachers of the law muttered, "This man welcomes sinners and eats[2] with them."

Then Jesus told them this parable:

"Suppose one of you has a hundred sheep and loses one of them. Does he not leave the ninety-nine in the open country and go after the lost sheep until he finds it? And when he finds it, he joyfully puts it on his shoulders and goes home. Then he calls his friends and neighbors together and says, 'Rejoice with me; I have found my lost sheep.' I tell you that in the same way there will be more rejoicing in heaven over one sinner who repents than over ninety-nine righteous persons who do not need to repent."

"Or suppose a woman has ten silver coins and loses one. Does she not light a lamp, sweep the house and search carefully until she finds it? And when she finds it, she calls her friends and neighbors together and says, 'Rejoice with me; I have found my lost coin.' In the same way, I tell you, there is rejoicing in the presence of the angels of God over one sinner who repents."

Explanatory Notes

[1]This and the following four stories (Luke 15:3–16:9) are called parables. They are stories about everyday and ordinary events. But Jesus used parables to teach about God and His kingdom. Parables are often called earthly stories with heavenly meanings. [2]Jesus had accepted invitations to their houses and eaten meals there, which went against Jewish custom.

"Rejoice with me!"

For Reflection

1. What criticism led Jesus to tell parables about the lost sheep and lost coin?
2. What do the shepherd and the woman do in the stories? Why do they rejoice?
3. Are you one of the lost sheep our Shepherd came to find? Why or why not?

Words to Remember

"For this is what the Sovereign LORD says: "I myself will search for My sheep and look after them." *Ezekiel 34:11*

The Lost[1] Son

Luke 15

Jesus continued:

"There was a man who had two sons. The younger one said to his father, 'Father, give me my share of the estate.' So he divided his property between them.

"Not long after that, the younger son got together all he had, set off for a distant country and there squandered his wealth in wild living. After he had spent everything, there was a severe famine[2] in that whole country, and he began to be in need. So he went and hired himself out to a citizen of that country, who sent him to his fields to feed pigs. He longed to fill his stomach with the pods that the pigs were eating, but no one gave him anything.

"When he came to his senses,[3] he said, 'How many of my father's hired men have food to spare, and here I am starving to death! I will set out and go back to my father and say to him: Father, I have sinned against heaven and against you. I am no longer worthy to be called your son; make me like one of your hired men.' So he got up and went to his father.

"But while he was still a long way off, his father saw him and was filled with compassion for him; he ran to his son, threw his arms around him and kissed him. The son said to him, 'Father, I have sinned against heaven and against you. I am no longer worthy to be called your son.' But the father said to his servants, 'Quick! Bring the best robe[4] and put it on him. Put a ring on his finger and sandals on his feet. Bring the fattened calf and kill it. Let's have a feast and celebrate. For this son of mine was dead and is alive again; he was lost and is found.' So they began to celebrate."

Explanatory Notes

[1]This parable is sometimes called "The Prodigal Son." A prodigal is a reckless, careless, wasteful person. [2]Shortage of food. [3]Realizing what he had done wrong. [4]A white embroidered garment, worn on special occasions.

His father saw him and was filled with compassion.

For Reflection
1. What words would you use to describe the father in the story?
2. Much like the lost son, we don't deserve to be called children of our heavenly Father. Why?
3. What did our heavenly Father do for us so that we might live as His children?

Words to Remember

In the same way, I tell you, there is rejoicing in the presence of the angels of God over one sinner who repents. *Luke 15:10*

157

The Foolish Rich Man

Luke 12

Jesus said to His disciples, "Watch out! Be on your guard against all kinds of greed;[1] a man's life does not consist in the abundance of his possessions."

And he told them this parable: "The ground of a certain rich man produced a good crop. He thought to himself, 'What shall I do? I have no place to store my crops.'

"Then he said, 'This is what I'll do. I will tear down my barns and build bigger ones, and there I will store all my grain and my goods. And I'll say to myself, "You have plenty of good things laid up for many years. Take life easy; eat, drink and be merry." '

"But God said to him, 'You fool![2] This very night your life will be demanded from you. Then who will get what you have prepared for yourself?'

"This is how it will be with anyone who stores up things for himself but is not rich toward God."

Then Jesus said to His disciples: "Therefore I tell you, do not worry about your life, what you will eat; or about your body, what you will wear. Life is more than food, and the body more than clothes. But seek His kingdom, and these things will be given to you as well."

Explanatory Notes
[1]Selfish desire to have more and more money and possessions. [2]God speaks His word of judgment.

"A man's life does not consist in the abundance of his possessions."

For Reflection
1. What sin does Jesus' story warn against?
2. What does it mean to seek God's kingdom?
3. What does Jesus also promise to those who seek His kingdom?

Words to Remember

Seek first His kingdom and His righteousness, and all these things will be given to you as well. *Matthew 6:33*

159

The Pharisee and the Tax Collector

Luke 18

To some who were confident of their own righteousness[1] and looked down on everybody else, Jesus told this parable:

"Two men went up to the temple to pray, one a Pharisee[2] and the other a tax collector.[3] The Pharisee stood up and prayed about himself: 'God, I thank you that I am not like other men—robbers, evildoers, adulterers[4]—or even like this tax collector. I fast twice a week and give a tenth of all I get.'

"But the tax collector stood at a distance. He would not even look up to heaven, but beat his breast[5] and said, 'God, have mercy on me, a sinner.'

"I tell you that this man, rather than the other, went home justified[6] before God. For everyone who exalts[7] himself will be humbled,[8] and he who humbles himself will be exalted.

Explanatory Notes

[1]Being just and holy before God. [2]One of the religious leaders, who considered themselves very righteous. [3]Considered by most people as being very low and dishonest. [4]People who sin against the Sixth Commandment and marriage. [5]Struck with his hand as a sign of sorrow. [6]With his sins forgiven. [7]Thinks himself better than others. [8]Brought low.

Two men went up to the temple to pray.

For Reflection
1. Which of the two men evidenced faith in God, trusting in His grace and goodness for salvation?
2. How do we know that God listened to the prayer of the tax collector?
3. What Good News does God have for all who, burdened by sin, pray the prayer of the tax collector?

Words to Remember

For we maintain that a man is justified by faith apart from observing the law. *Romans 3:28*

The Good Samaritan

Luke 10

On one occasion an expert in the law stood up to test Jesus. "Teacher," he asked, "what must I do to inherit eternal life?"

"What is written in the Law?" He replied. "How do you read it?"

He answered: "'Love the Lord your God with all your heart and with all your soul and with all your strength and with all your mind'; and, 'Love your neighbor as yourself.'"

"You have answered correctly," Jesus replied. "Do this and you will live."

But he wanted to justify himself, so he asked Jesus, "And who is my neighbor?"

In reply Jesus said: "A man was going down from Jerusalem to Jericho, when he fell into the hands of robbers. They stripped him of his clothes, beat him and went away, leaving him half dead. A priest happened to be going down the same road, and when he saw the man, he passed by on the other side. So too, a Levite,[1] when he came to the place and saw him, passed by on the other side. But a Samaritan,[2] as he traveled, came where the man was; and when he saw him, he took pity on him. He went to him and bandaged his wounds, pouring on oil and wine. Then he put the man on his own donkey, took him to an inn and took care of him. The next day he took out two silver coins[3] and gave them to the innkeeper. 'Look after him,' he said, 'and when I return, I will reimburse you for any extra expense you may have.'

"Which of these three do you think was a neighbor to the man who fell into the hands of robbers?"

The expert in the law replied, "The one who had mercy on him."

Jesus told him, "Go and do likewise."

Explanatory Notes

[1]Another type of priest. [2]Man from Samaria, who was considered an outcast. [3]Two days' wages, which would keep a man up to two months in an inn.

"Who is my neighbor?"

For Reflection

1. Which words summarize the Law of God that Jesus lived in our place in order to earn heaven for us?
2. Who is our neighbor? Give examples that show how to be a Christian neighbor.
3. Which of the characters in this story reminds us most of Jesus? Why?

Words to Remember

We love because He first loved us. *1 John 4:19*

163

The Triumphal Entry[1]

Matthew 21

As they approached Jerusalem and came to Bethphage on the Mount of Olives, Jesus sent two disciples, saying to them, "Go to the village ahead of you, and at once you will find a donkey tied there, with her colt by her. Untie them and bring them to Me. If anyone says anything to you, tell him that the Lord needs them, and he will send them right away."

This took place to fulfill what was spoken through the prophet:[2] "Say to the Daughter of Zion,[3] 'See, your king comes to you, gentle and riding on a donkey, on a colt, the foal[4] of a donkey.'"

The disciples went and did as Jesus had instructed them. They brought the donkey and the colt, placed their cloaks on them, and Jesus sat on them.

A very large crowd spread their cloaks on the road, while others cut branches from the trees and spread them on the road. The crowds that went ahead of Him and those that followed shouted, "Hosanna[5] to the Son of David! Blessed is He who comes in the name of the Lord! Hosanna in the highest!"

Explanatory Notes

[1]Jesus and His disciples were now on the way to Jerusalem, where He was about to begin His great suffering that ended in His death on the cross for our salvation. [2]See Zechariah 9:9. [3]The city of Jerusalem, which stands for the Christian church. [4]The young. [5]Hosanna is Hebrew for "Save us!" which became an exclamation of praise.

"Hosanna in the highest!"

For Reflection
1. What Old Testament prophecy did Jesus fulfill in this account?
2. How did the people worship Jesus?
3. How and why do we worship Jesus today?

Words to Remember

Lift up your heads, O you gates; be lifted up, you ancient doors, that the King of glory may come in. *Psalm 24:7*

The Anointing

Mark 14; John 12

Six days before the Passover, Jesus arrived at Bethany, where Lazarus lived, whom Jesus had raised from the dead. Here a dinner was given in Jesus' honor. Martha served, while Lazarus was among those reclining at the table with him. Then Mary took about a pint of pure nard, an expensive perfume[1]; she poured it on Jesus' feet and wiped His feet with her hair. And the house was filled with the fragrance of the perfume.

Some of those present were saying indignantly to one another, "Why this waste of perfume? It could have been sold for more than a year's wages and the money given to the poor." And they rebuked her harshly.

"Leave her alone," said Jesus. "Why are you bothering her? She has done a beautiful thing to Me. The poor you will always have with you, and you can help them any time you want. But you will not always have Me. She did what she could. She poured perfume on My body beforehand to prepare for My burial. I tell you the truth, wherever the gospel is preached throughout the world, what she has done will also be told, in memory of her."

Then Judas Iscariot, one of the Twelve, went to the chief priests to betray Jesus to them. They were delighted to hear this and promised to give him money. So he watched for an opportunity to hand Him over.

Explanatory Notes

[1]Also known as spikenard, the plant was imported from the Himalayas and made into an ointment.

She wiped His feet with her hair.

For Reflection

1. Describe Mary's act of worship.
2. What had Jesus done for Mary and her family?
3. What good things has Jesus done for you and your family?

Words to Remember

Praise the Lord, O my soul, and forget not all His benefits—who forgives all your sins and heals all your diseases. *Psalm 103:3*

The Last Judgment

Matthew 25

Jesus said: "When the Son of Man comes in His glory, and all the angels with Him, He will sit on His throne in heavenly glory. All the nations[1] will be gathered before Him, and He will separate the people one from another as a shepherd separates the sheep from the goats. He will put the sheep on His right and the goats on His left.

"Then the King will say to those on His right, 'Come, you who are blessed by My Father; take your inheritance,[2] the kingdom prepared for you. For I was hungry and you gave Me something to eat, I was thirsty and you gave Me something to drink, I was a stranger and you invited Me in, I needed clothes and you clothed Me, I was sick and you looked after Me, I was in prison and you came to visit Me.'

"Then the righteous will answer Him, 'Lord, when did we see You hungry and feed You, or thirsty and give You something to drink? When did we see You a stranger and invite You in, or needing clothes and clothe You? When did we see You sick or in prison and go to visit You?'

"The King will reply, 'I tell you the truth, whatever you did for one of the least of these brothers of Mine, you did for Me.'

"Then He will say to those on His left, 'Depart from Me, you who are cursed, into the eternal fire prepared for the devil and his angels. For I was hungry and you gave Me nothing to eat, I was thirsty and you gave Me nothing to drink, I was a stranger and you did not invite Me in, I needed clothes and you did not clothe Me, I was sick and in prison and you did not look after Me.'

"They also will answer, 'Lord, when did we see You hungry or thirsty or a stranger or needing clothes or sick or in prison, and did not help You?'

"He will reply, 'I tell you the truth, whatever you did not do for one of the least of these, you did not do for Me.'

"Then they will go away to eternal punishment, but the righteous to eternal life."

Explanatory Notes
[1] All people, both living and dead. [2] Because you are My children, receive the share I promised you.

"He will sit on His throne in heavenly glory."

For Reflection

1. Who will come before Jesus and the holy angels on judgment day?
2. By what evidence will Jesus identify those who have lived in faith in Him?
3. The people on the King's right showed mercy to those less fortunate than they. How has Jesus shown mercy to us?

Words to Remember

And you will receive a rich welcome into the eternal kingdom of our Lord and Savior Jesus Christ. *2 Peter 1:11*

The Lord's Supper[1]

Luke 22

Jesus said to His disciples, "As you know, the Passover is two days away[2]—and the Son of Man will be handed[3] over to be crucified."

Then Satan entered Judas, called Iscariot, one of the Twelve. He went to the chief priests and asked, "What are you willing to give me if I hand Him over to you?"[4] So they counted out for him thirty silver coins.[5] From then on Judas watched for an opportunity to hand Him over.

Jesus sent Peter and John, saying, "Go and make preparations for us to eat the Passover." So they prepared the Passover.

When the hour[6] came, Jesus and His disciples reclined at the table. And He said to them, "I have eagerly desired to eat this Passover with you before I suffer."

While they were eating, Jesus took bread, gave thanks and broke it, and gave it to His disciples, saying, "Take and eat; this is My body, which is for you; do this in remembrance of Me." In the same way, after supper He took the cup, gave thanks, and offered it to them, saying, "Drink from it, all of you. This cup is the new covenant[7] in My blood, which is poured out for many for the forgiveness of sins; do this, whenever you drink it, in remembrance of Me."

Explanatory Notes

[1]This and the following seven stories are an account of the Savior's Passion, relating the events that happened from late Thursday afternoon of Holy Week till Saturday evening. [2]The Passover was celebrated on the fourteenth day of the first month, called Nisan (about March-April). [3]Secretly given up to the enemy. [4]"I will see that He falls into your hands." [5]About four months' wages. [6]Evening. [7]God's solemn pledge and agreement to save His people in the coming Messiah (see Jeremiah 31:31–34).

"This cup is poured out for many for the forgiveness of sins."

For Reflection

1. Tell how Judas turned his back on Jesus.

2. Jesus and His disciples assembled to eat the Passover meal. Compare the Passover meal with the new meal Jesus gave to His followers? What does Jesus give us through the Lord's Supper?

3. Why did Jesus give His body and blood? How did He do it?

Words to Remember

For whenever you eat this bread and drink this cup, you proclaim the Lord's death until He comes. *1 Corinthians 11:2*

Jesus in Gethsemane

Matthew 26; Luke 22

Jesus went out[1] to the Mount of Olives, and His disciples followed Him. Then Jesus told them, "This very night you will all fall away on account of Me."

Peter replied, "Even if all fall away on account of You, I never will."

"I tell you the truth," Jesus answered, "this very night, before the rooster crows, you will disown Me three times."

They went to a place called Gethsemane, and Jesus said to His disciples, "Sit here while I pray." He took Peter, James and John along with Him, and He began to be deeply distressed and troubled. "My soul is overwhelmed with sorrow to the point of death," He said to them. "Stay here and keep watch."

Going a little farther, He fell with His face to the ground and prayed. "Abba, Father," He said, "everything is possible for You. Take this cup[2] from Me. Yet not what I will, but what You will." Then He returned to His disciples and found them sleeping. "Simon," He said to Peter, "are you asleep? Could you not keep watch for one hour? Watch and pray so that you will not fall into temptation. The spirit is willing, but the body is weak."

He went away a second time and prayed, "My Father, if it is not possible for this cup to be taken away unless I drink it, may Your will be done."

When He came back, He again found them sleeping. So He left them and went away once more and prayed the third time, saying the same thing. An angel from heaven appeared to Him and strengthened Him. And being in anguish,[3] He prayed more earnestly, and His sweat was like drops of blood falling to the ground.

When He rose from prayer and went back to the disciples, He found them asleep, exhausted from sorrow. He said to them, "Are you still sleeping? Rise, let us go! Here comes My betrayer!"

Explanatory Notes

[1]From where they had eaten the Passover. [2]He compared His suffering with a bitter drink. [3]Very great suffering, close to death.

"May Your will be done."

For Reflection

1. How does Jesus' prayer to His heavenly Father show Him to be true man? What evidence do you find in this account that Jesus is true God?
2. What did Jesus ask His disciples to do? Why were they unable to do what He asked?
3. Why was Jesus willing to submit to God's will, even though He knew the enormous pain and suffering He would have to endure?

Words to Remember

Surely He took up our infirmities and carried our sorrows. *Isaiah 53:4*

Jesus Is Betrayed and Arrested

Matthew 26; John 18

While He was still speaking, Judas, one of the Twelve, arrived. With him was a large crowd sent from the chief priests and the elders of the people. They were carrying torches, lanterns and weapons. Now the betrayer had arranged a signal with them: "The one I kiss is the man; arrest Him."

Jesus, knowing all that was going to happen to Him, went out and asked them, "Who is it you want?"

"Jesus of Nazareth," they replied.

"I am He," Jesus said.

When Jesus said, "I am He," they drew back and fell to the ground. Again He asked them, "Who is it you want?"

And they said, "Jesus of Nazareth."

"I told you that I am He," Jesus answered. "If you are looking for Me, then let these men go."[1]

Going at once to Jesus, Judas said, "Greetings, Rabbi!"[2] and kissed Him. But Jesus asked him, "Judas, are you betraying the Son of Man with a kiss?" The men seized Jesus and arrested Him. Then Simon Peter, who had a sword, drew it and struck the high priest's servant, cutting off his right ear.

"Put your sword back in its place," Jesus said to him, "for all who draw the sword will die by the sword. Do you think I cannot call on my Father, and He will at once put at my disposal more than twelve legions of angels?"[3] And He touched the man's ear and healed him. Then everyone deserted Him and fled.

Explanatory Notes
[1] The disciples. [2] Hebrew for "Teacher." [3] 72,000.

"Judas, are you betraying the Son of Man with a kiss?"

For Reflection

1. Why do you suppose Judas was willing to betray Jesus?
2. Why didn't Jesus call to His Father and ask for the assistance of angels?
3. How did Jesus show His love and care for the servant of the high priest?

Words to Remember

Even My close friend, whom I trusted, he who shared my bread, has lifted up his heel against Me. *Psalm 41:9*

Jesus before the Sanhedrin

Matthew 26; John 18

Then the detachment of soldiers with its commander and the Jewish officials arrested Jesus. They bound Him and took Him to Caiaphas, the high priest, where the teachers of the law and the elders had assembled.

The high priest[1] questioned Jesus about His disciples and His teaching.

"I have spoken openly to the world," Jesus replied. "I said nothing in secret. Ask those who heard Me."

When Jesus said this, one of the officials nearby struck Him in the face. "Is this the way You answer the high priest?" he demanded.

"If I said something wrong," Jesus replied, "testify[2] as to what is wrong. But if I spoke the truth, why did you strike Me?"

The chief priests and the whole Sanhedrin[3] were looking for evidence against Jesus so that they could put Him to death, but they did not find any. Many testified falsely against Him, but their statements did not agree.

The high priest said to Him, "I charge you under oath by the living God: Tell us if You are the Christ, the Son of God."

"Yes, it is as you say," Jesus replied.

Then the high priest tore his clothes and said, "He has spoken blasphemy![4] Why do we need any more witnesses? Look, now you have heard the blasphemy. What do you think?"

"He is worthy of death," they answered.

Then some began to spit at Him; they blindfolded Him, struck Him with their fists, and said, "Prophesy to us, Christ. Who hit you?" And the guards took Him and beat Him.

Explanatory Notes

[1]Jesus was taken for questioning to both Caiaphas and Annas, Caiaphas' father-in-law, who many thought to be the true high priest. This series of questioning was with Annas. See John 18:12–14, 19–24. [2]Prove. [3]The highest court of the Jewish church. [4]He has mocked God.

The high priest questioned Jesus.

For Reflection

1. How does Jesus respond when asked whether He is the Christ, the Son of God?
2. Jesus was accused of committing blasphemy. Who was actually guilty of committing blasphemy?
3. If Christ was the Son of God, why did He endure the abuse at the hands of His opponents?

Words to Remember

I offered my back to those who beat Me, My cheeks to those who pulled out My beard; I did not hide My face from mocking and spitting. *Isaiah 50:*

177

Peter Disowns Jesus; Judas Dies

Luke 22; Matthew 26–27

Peter followed Him at a distance, right into the courtyard[1] of the high priest. It was cold, and the servants and officials stood around a fire they had made to keep warm. Peter sat down with them to see the outcome.[2] "You are not one of His disciples, are you?" the girl at the door asked Peter.

He replied, "I am not."

Then he went out to the gateway, where another girl saw him and said to the people there, "This fellow was with Jesus of Nazareth." Someone else saw him and said, "You also are one of them."

"I am not!" Peter replied.

After a little while, those standing near said to Peter, "Surely you are one of them, for you are a Galilean—your accent gives you away." One of the high priest's servants, a relative of the man whose ear Peter had cut off, challenged him, "Didn't I see you with Him in the olive grove?"

He began to call down curses on himself, and he swore to them, "I don't know this man you're talking about."

Just as he was speaking, the rooster crowed. The Lord turned and looked straight at Peter. Then Peter remembered the word the Lord had spoken to him: "Before the rooster crows today, you will disown Me three times." And he went outside and wept bitterly.

When Judas, who had betrayed Him, saw that Jesus was condemned, he was seized with remorse[3] and returned the thirty silver coins to the chief priests and the elders. "I have sinned," he said, "for I have betrayed innocent blood."

"What is that to us?" they replied. "That's your responsibility."

So Judas threw the money into the temple and left. Then he went away and hanged himself; and his body burst open and all his intestines spilled out.[4]

Explanatory Notes

[1]Courtyard of his residence. [2]What would happen to the Lord. [3]Felt sorry. [4]See Acts 1:18. After he hung himself, the body fell—either because of decay or because someone cut him down—then broke open because of its decomposed condition.

The courtyard of the high priest ... around a fire they had made to keep warm.

For Reflection

1. Peter followed Jesus into the High Priest's palace. Yet he denied knowing Jesus. Why?
2. Both Peter and Judas became sorry for what they had done. In what ways was their sorrow different?
3. Because of our sinful nature, we, like both Peter and Judas, are guilty of betraying the Lord. Judas lost hope because of his guilt. Is there reason for us to lose hope? Why not?

Words to Remember

Godly sorrow brings repentance that leads to salvation and leaves no regret, but worldly sorrow brings death. *2 Corinthians 7:10*

Jesus before Pilate

Matthew 27; John 18

Very early in the morning, the chief priests, with the elders, the teachers of the law and the whole Sanhedrin bound Jesus, led Him away and handed Him over to Pilate, the Roman governor. Pilate came out to them and asked, "What charges are you bringing against this man?" And they began to accuse Him, saying, "We have found this Man subverting[1] our nation. He claims to be Christ, a king."

So Pilate asked Jesus, "Are You the king of the Jews?"

Jesus said, "My kingdom is not of this world."

"You are a king, then!" said Pilate.

Jesus answered, "You are right in saying I am a king. In fact, for this reason I was born, and for this I came into the world, to testify to the truth. Everyone on the side of truth listens to Me."

Pilate called together the chief priests, the rulers and the people, and said to them, "I find no basis for a charge against Him. Therefore, I will punish Him and then release Him." But they kept shouting, "Crucify Him! Crucify Him!"

Then Pilate took Jesus and had Him flogged.[2] They stripped Him and put a scarlet robe on Him, and then twisted together a crown of thorns and set it on His head. They put a staff in His right hand and knelt in front of Him and mocked Him. "Hail, king of the Jews!" they said. They spit on Him, and took the staff and struck Him on the head again and again.

Once more Pilate came out and said to the Jews, "Look, I am bringing Him out to you to let you know that I find no basis for a charge against Him." When Jesus came out wearing the crown of thorns and the purple robe, Pilate said to them, "Here is the man!"

As soon as the chief priests and their officials saw Him, they shouted, "Crucify! Crucify!"

Pilate took water and washed his hands in front of the crowd. "I am innocent of this man's blood," he said. "It is your responsibility!" All the people answered, "Let His blood be on us and on our children!"

Finally Pilate handed Him over to be crucified.

Explanatory Notes
[1]Turning the people against the government. [2]Whipped.

"Are You the king of the Jews?"

For Reflection
1. Describe how Jesus suffered under Pontius Pilate.
2. Why did Pilate sentence Jesus to be crucified even though he knew Jesus to be innocent?
3. The people said to Pilate, "Let [Jesus'] blood be on us and on our children." What does it mean for believers to be covered with the blood of Christ?

Words to Remember
But if we walk in the light, as He is in the light, we have fellowship with one another, and the blood of Jesus, His Son, purifies us from all sin. *1 John 1:7*

181

Jesus Is Crucified

Luke 23; John 19

Then the governor's soldiers took Jesus and put His own clothes on Him and led Him away to crucify Him. Carrying His own cross,[1] He went out to the place called Golgotha.[2]

Here they crucified Him, and with Him two others—one on each side and Jesus in the middle. It was the third hour[3] when they crucified Him. Jesus said, "Father, forgive them, for they do not know what they are doing."

When Jesus saw His mother standing near the cross, and the disciple whom He loved[4] standing nearby, He said to His mother, "Dear woman, here is your son," and to the disciple, "Here is your mother." From that time on, this disciple took her into his home.

Those who passed by hurled insults at Him. One of the criminals who hung there hurled insults at Him: "Aren't You the Christ? Save Yourself and us!" But the other criminal rebuked him. "We are punished justly, for we are getting what our deeds deserve. But this man has done nothing wrong." Then he said, "Jesus, remember me when You come into Your kingdom."

Jesus answered him, "I tell you the truth, today you will be with Me in paradise."

At the sixth hour darkness came over the whole land until the ninth hour.[5] And at the ninth hour Jesus cried out in a loud voice, "My God, My God, why have You forsaken Me?"

Explanatory Notes

[1]Somewhere along the way, Simon of Cyrene took Jesus' cross (See Mark 15:21), probably because Jesus was weakened by the flogging. [2]Aramaic for "the skull." Also called Calvary. [3]Nine o'clock in the morning. [4]John. [5]From noon until 3 P.M.

Carrying His own cross, He went out to Golgotha.

For Reflection
1. What do we learn about Jesus from the words He spoke on the cross?
2. What miraculous events occurred to indicate the significance of Jesus' death?
3. What does it mean to you personally that Jesus died on a cross long ago on Calvary?

Words to Remember

But He was pierced for our transgressions, He was crushed for our iniquities; the punishment that brought us peace was upon Him, and by His wounds we are healed. *Isaiah 53:5*

Jesus Dies and Is Buried

John 19

Later, knowing that all was now completed, Jesus said, "I am thirsty." A jar of wine vinegar was there, so they soaked a sponge in it, put the sponge on a stalk of the hyssop plant, and lifted it to Jesus' lips. When He had received the drink, Jesus said, "It is finished."

Jesus called out with a loud voice, "Father, into Your hands I commit My spirit." With that, He bowed His head and gave up His spirit. The centurion who stood there in front of Jesus said, "Surely this man was the Son of God!"

Because the Jews did not want the bodies left on the crosses during the Sabbath, they asked Pilate to have the legs broken and the bodies taken down. The soldiers therefore came and broke the legs of the first man who had been crucified with Jesus, and then those of the other. But when they came to Jesus and found that He was already dead, they did not break His legs. Instead, one of the soldiers pierced Jesus' side with a spear, bringing a sudden flow of blood and water.[1]

As evening approached, Joseph of Arimathea, a prominent member of the Council, who had not consented to their decision and action[2] being a disciple of Jesus, went boldly to Pilate and asked for Jesus' body. Pilate ordered that it be given to him. He was accompanied by Nicodemus,[3] who brought a mixture of myrrh and aloes.[4] Taking Jesus' body, the two of them wrapped it, with the spices, in strips of linen.

At the place where Jesus was crucified, there was a garden, and in the garden a new tomb, cut out of rock. They laid Jesus there, rolled a big stone in front of the entrance to the tomb, and went away.

The next day, the chief priests and the Pharisees went to Pilate. "Sir," they said, "we remember that while He was still alive that deceiver said, 'After three days I will rise again.' So give the order for the tomb to be made secure until the third day. Otherwise, His disciples may come and steal the body and tell the people that He has been raised from the dead."

"Take a guard," Pilate answered. So they went and made the tomb secure by putting a seal on the stone and posting the guard.

Explanatory Notes

[1]The result of the spear piercing the heart and the sac around the heart. [2]Had not, like the others, condemned Jesus to death. [3]Also a secret disciple of Jesus. [4]Expensive spices, used for embalming.

"It is finished."

For Reflection

1. How did the soldier make sure that Jesus was indeed dead?
2. Describe the burial of Jesus.
3. Why was it so important that Jesus physically die? (See "Words to Remember.")

Words to Remember

For we know that our old self was crucified with Him so that the body of sin might be done away with, that we should no longer be slaves to sin—because anyone who has died has been freed from sin. *Romans 6:6–7*

The Resurrection of Christ

Matthew 28; Mark 16

When the Sabbath was over, Mary Magdalene, Mary the mother of James, and Salome bought spices so that they might go to anoint Jesus' body. Very early on the first day of the week, just after sunrise, they were on their way to the tomb.

There was a violent earthquake, for an angel of the Lord came down from heaven and, going to the tomb, rolled back the stone and sat on it. His appearance was like lightning, and his clothes were white as snow. The guards were so afraid of him that they shook and became like dead men.[1]

The women asked each other, "Who will roll the stone away from the entrance of the tomb?" But when they looked up, they saw that the stone, which was very large, had been rolled away. When Mary Magdalene saw that the stone had been removed from the entrance, she went running to Simon Peter and the other disciple, the one Jesus loved, and said, "They have taken the Lord out of the tomb, and we don't know where they have put Him!"

The other women, as they entered the tomb, saw a young man dressed in a white robe sitting on the right side, and they were alarmed. "Don't be alarmed," he said. "You are looking for Jesus the Nazarene, who was crucified. He has risen! He is not here. See the place where they laid Him. But go, tell His disciples and Peter, 'He is going ahead of you into Galilee. There you will see Him, just as He told you.'"

So the women hurried away from the tomb, afraid yet filled with joy.

Explanatory Notes
[1]Fell unconscious.

He has risen!

For Reflection
1. Tell about the actions of the angel on Easter morning.
2. How did the women respond to the message of the angel?
3. What does the message of the angel mean for us today?

Words to Remember

[He] was declared with power to be the Son of God by His resurrection from the dead: Jesus Christ our Lord. *Romans 1:4*

The First Appearances of the Risen Lord

Matthew 28; John 20

The women ran to tell His disciples what the angel had told them. Suddenly Jesus met them. "Greetings," He said. They came to Him, clasped His feet and worshiped Him.

Then Jesus said to them, "Do not be afraid. Go and tell My brothers to go to Galilee; there they will see Me."

While the women were on their way, some of the guards went into the city and reported to the chief priests everything that had happened. When the chief priests had met with the elders and devised a plan, they gave the soldiers a large sum of money, telling them, "You are to say, 'His disciples came during the night and stole Him away while we were asleep.' If this report gets to the governor, we will satisfy him and keep you out of trouble."

So the soldiers took the money and did as they were instructed.

But Mary[1] stood outside the tomb crying. She turned around and saw Jesus standing there, but she did not realize that it was Jesus.

"Woman," He said, "why are you crying? Who is it you are looking for?"

Thinking He was the gardener, she said, "Sir, if you have carried Him away, tell me where you have put Him, and I will get Him."

Jesus said to her, "Mary."

She turned toward Him and cried out in Aramaic, "Rabboni!" (which means Teacher).

Jesus said, "Do not hold on to Me, for I have not yet returned to the Father. Go instead to My brothers and tell them, 'I am returning to My Father and your Father, to My God and your God.'"

Mary Magdalene went to the disciples with the news: "I have seen the Lord!" And she told them that He had said these things to her.

Explanatory Notes
[1]Mary Magdalene.

"I have seen the Lord!"

For Reflection
1. Describe Jesus' first resurrection appearances.
2. How did the leaders of the people attempt to "cover up" the good news of Jesus' resurrection?
3. Why are the appearances of Jesus after His resurrection so important?

Words to Remember
And if Christ has not been raised, your faith is futile; you are still in your sins. *1 Corinthians 15:17*

Christ Appears to His Disciples

Matthew 28; John 20

On the evening of that first day of the week,[1] when the disciples were together, with the doors locked for fear of the Jews, Jesus came and stood among them and said, "Peace be with you!"

They were startled and frightened, thinking they saw a ghost.

He said to them, "Why are you troubled, and why do doubts rise in your minds? Look at My hands and My feet. It is I Myself! Touch Me and see; a ghost does not have flesh and bones, as you see I have." When He had said this, He showed them His hands and feet.

The disciples were overjoyed when they saw the Lord.

Again Jesus said, "Peace be with you! As the Father has sent Me, I am sending you." And with that He breathed on them and said, "Receive the Holy Spirit. If you forgive anyone his sins, they are forgiven; if you do not forgive them, they are not forgiven."

Then the eleven disciples went to Galilee, to the mountain where Jesus had told them to go. When they saw Him, they worshiped Him; but some doubted. Then Jesus came to them and said, "All authority in heaven and on earth has been given to Me. Therefore go and make disciples of all nations, baptizing them in the name of the Father and of the Son and of the Holy Spirit, and teaching them to obey everything I have commanded you. And surely I am with you always, to the very end of the age."[2]

Explanatory Notes

[1] Easter Sunday, the day on which Jesus had risen. [2] This is Christ's great commission (command) to all Christians to proclaim the Gospel to all peoples.

Jesus said, "Peace be with you!"

For Reflection
1. Jesus twice tells His disciples, "Peace be with you!" How is peace related to Christ's resurrection?
2. Why did Jesus invite the disciples to look at His hands and feet?
3. Jesus promised the disciples His power and His presence in the new life they were to live for Him. Describe the goals and objectives God brings to the lives of all who love and trust in Jesus the risen Savior.

Words to Remember
Blessed are those who have not seen and yet have believed. *John 20:29*

The Ascension[1]

Acts 1

Jesus, after His suffering, showed Himself to the apostles and gave many convincing proofs[2] that He was alive. He appeared to them over a period of forty days and spoke about the kingdom of God.[3]

On one occasion, while He was eating with them, He gave them this command: "Do not leave Jerusalem, but wait for the gift My Father promised, which you have heard Me speak about. For John baptized with water, but in a few days you will be baptized with the Holy Spirit."

After the Lord Jesus had spoken to them, He led them out to the vicinity of Bethany, and He lifted up His hands and blessed them. While He was blessing them, He left them and was taken up into heaven, and a cloud hid Him from their sight, and He sat at the right hand of God.[4]

They were looking intently up into the sky as He was going, when suddenly two men dressed in white stood beside them. "Men of Galilee," they said, "why do you stand here looking into the sky? This same Jesus, who has been taken from you into heaven, will come back in the same way you have seen Him go into heaven."[5]

Then they worshiped Him and returned to Jerusalem with great joy.

Explanatory Notes

[1]Going into heaven. [2]Evidence that is certain. The resurrection of Jesus is sure; it cannot be denied. [3]He taught them many things that they needed to know in order to carry on His work after He would be gone. [4]A position of authority. [5]Jesus will return visibly on Judgment Day, even as He ascended visibly.

He left them and was taken up into heaven.

For Reflection

1. What gift did Jesus tell the disciples to wait for in Jerusalem?
2. What did the angels promise the disciples after Jesus ascended into heaven?
3. Although Jesus ascended into heaven, He has not been "taken away" from us. Explain.

Words to Remember

But to each one of us grace has been given as Christ apportioned it. This is why it says: "When He ascended on high, He led captives in His train and gave gifts to men." *Ephesians 4:7–8*

193

The Holy Spirit Comes at Pentecost

Acts 2

When the day of Pentecost[1] came, they were all together in one place. Suddenly a sound like the blowing of a violent wind came from heaven and filled the whole house where they were sitting. They saw what seemed to be tongues of fire[2] that separated and came to rest on each of them. All of them were filled with the Holy Spirit and began to speak in other tongues[3] as the Spirit enabled them.

Now there were staying in Jerusalem God-fearing[4] Jews from every nation under heaven. When they heard this sound,[5] a crowd came together in bewilderment. Utterly amazed, they asked: "Are not all these men who are speaking Galileans? Then how is it that each of us hears them declaring the wonders of God in our own native language?"

Some, however, made fun of them and said, "They have had too much wine."

Then Peter stood up with the Eleven, raised his voice and addressed the crowd: "Men of Israel, listen to this: Jesus of Nazareth was a man accredited by God to you by miracles.[6] You put Him to death by nailing Him to the cross. But God raised Him from the dead, freeing Him from the agony of death, because it was impossible for death to keep its hold on Him. Therefore let all Israel be assured of this: God has made this Jesus, whom you crucified, both Lord and Christ."

When the people heard this, they were cut to the heart[7] and said to Peter and the other apostles, "Brothers, what shall we do?"

Peter replied, "Repent and be baptized, every one of you, in the name of Jesus Christ for the forgiveness of your sins. And you will receive the gift of the Holy Spirit. The promise is for you and your children and for all who are far off—for all whom the Lord our God will call."[8]

Those who accepted his message were baptized, and about three thousand were added to their number that day.

Explanatory Notes

[1]Pentecost means fiftieth; it was celebrated fifty days after the Passover; see Leviticus 23. [2]Fire in the form of split flames. [3]Languages. [4]Very religious. [5]Of wind and everyone speaking. [6]The works done by Jesus were signs that He is the Messiah, the Savior, blessed by God. [7]Reflects both belief in Jesus, and regret for rejecting Him in the past. [8]All people of all times and places.

All of them were filled with the Holy Spirit.

For Reflection

1. In what ways did the Holy Spirit make His presence known at Pentecost?
2. Describe Peter's Pentecost sermon and its result.
3. In what ways does the Holy Spirit come to and work in the lives of God's people today?

Words to Remember

"And afterward, I will pour out My Spirit on all people." *Joel 2:28*

The Crippled Beggar Is Healed

Acts 3

One day Peter and John were going up to the temple at the time of prayer—at three in the afternoon. Now a man crippled from birth was being carried to the temple gate, where he was put every day to beg from those going into the temple courts. When he saw Peter and John about to enter, he asked them for money.

Peter said, "Look at us!"

So the man gave them his attention, expecting to get something from them.

Then Peter said, "Silver or gold I do not have, but what I have I give you. In the name of Jesus Christ of Nazareth, walk." Taking him by the right hand, he helped him up, and instantly the man's feet and ankles became strong. He jumped to his feet and began to walk. Then he went with them into the temple courts, walking and jumping, and praising God.

When all the people saw him walking and praising God, they were filled with wonder and amazement at what had happened to him.

While the beggar held on to Peter and John, all the people were astonished and came running to them. When Peter saw this, he said to them: "Men of Israel, why does this surprise you? Why do you stare at us as if by our own power or godliness we had made this man walk? The God of Abraham, Isaac and Jacob has glorified His servant Jesus. You handed Him over to be killed, and you disowned Him before Pilate. You disowned the Holy and Righteous One. You killed the Author of life, but God raised Him from the dead. We are witnesses of this. I know that you acted in ignorance, as did your leaders. Repent, then, and turn to God, so that your sins may be wiped out,[1] that times of refreshing may come from the Lord."

Many who heard the message believed, and the number of men grew to about five thousand.

Explanatory Notes
[1] Forgiven.

He went ... walking and jumping, and praising God.

For Reflection
1. Whom did Peter and John credit for the miraculous healing of the beggar?
2. How did Peter use the healing of the beggar to tell others about Jesus?
3. The beggar asked for money and received healing instead. In what unexpected ways has God in Christ blessed you?

Words to Remember
"I will heal My people and will let them enjoy abundant peace and security."
Jeremiah 33:6b

Stephen

Acts 6–7

Now Stephen,[1] a man full of God's grace and power, did great wonders and miraculous signs among the people. Opposition arose, however, from members of the Synagogue of the Freedmen.[2] These men began to argue with Stephen, but they could not stand up against his wisdom or the Spirit by whom he spoke. So they stirred up the people and seized Stephen and brought him before the Sanhedrin. They produced false witnesses, who testified, "This fellow never stops speaking against this holy place and against the law. For we have heard him say that this Jesus of Nazareth will destroy this place and change the customs[3] Moses handed down to us."

All who were sitting in the Sanhedrin looked intently at Stephen, and they saw that his face was like the face of an angel.

Then the high priest asked him, "Are these charges true?"

To this he replied: "You stiff-necked people, with uncircumcised hearts and ears![4] You are just like your fathers: You always resist the Holy Spirit! Was there ever a prophet your fathers did not persecute?[5] They even killed those who predicted the coming of the Righteous One. And now you have betrayed and murdered Him."

When they heard this, they were furious and gnashed their teeth at him.[6] But Stephen, full of the Holy Spirit, looked up to heaven. "Look," he said, "I see heaven open and the Son of Man standing at the right hand of God."

At this they all rushed at him, dragged him out of the city and began to stone him. Meanwhile, the witnesses laid their clothes[7] at the feet of a young man named Saul. While they were stoning him, Stephen prayed, "Lord Jesus, receive my spirit." Then he fell on his knees and cried out, "Lord, do not hold this sin against them."

When he had said this, he fell asleep.[8] And Saul was there, giving approval to his death. Godly men buried Stephen and mourned deeply for him.

Explanatory Notes

[1]One of the seven deacons of the congregation in Jerusalem. [2]Persons who had been freed from slavery. [3]Laws. [4]Wicked who refuse to repent. [5]Made life miserable for them and even killed them. [6]Because they were very angry. [7]Outer garments, cloaks. [8]Died.

"Lord, do not hold this sin against them."

For Reflection
1. Why was Stephen stoned to death?
2. What did Stephen pray as his enemies were killing him? Whose example was he following?
3. Describe the strength of Stephen's faith? How does God's Spirit help those who believe in Jesus when they face ridicule and opposition?

Words to Remember
"These are they who have come out of the great tribulation; they have washed their robes and made them white in the blood of the Lamb." *Revelation 7:14*

Philip and the Ethiopian

Acts 8

Now an angel of the Lord said to Philip, "Go south to the road—the desert road—that goes down from Jerusalem to Gaza."

So he started out, and on his way he met an Ethiopian eunuch, an important official in charge of all the treasury of Candace, queen of the Ethiopians. This man had gone to Jerusalem to worship,[1] and on his way home was sitting in his chariot reading the book of Isaiah the prophet.

The Spirit told Philip, "Go to that chariot and stay near it."

Then Philip ran up to the chariot and heard the man reading Isaiah the prophet. "Do you understand what you are reading?" Philip asked.

"How can I," he said, "unless someone explains it to me?" So he invited Philip to come up and sit with him.

The eunuch was reading this passage of Scripture:

> *"He was led like a sheep to the slaughter,*
> *and as a lamb before the shearer is silent,*
> *so He did not open His mouth.*
> *In His humiliation He was deprived of justice.*
> *Who can speak of His descendants?*
> *For His life was taken from the earth."*[2]

The eunuch asked Philip, "Tell me, please, who is the prophet talking about, himself or someone else?" Then Philip began with that very passage of Scripture and told him the good news about Jesus.

As they traveled along the road, they came to some water and the eunuch said, "Look, here is water. Why shouldn't I be baptized?"

And he gave orders to stop the chariot. Then both Philip and the eunuch went down into the water and Philip baptized him. When they came up out of the water, the Spirit of the Lord suddenly took Philip away, and the eunuch did not see him again, but went on his way rejoicing.

Explanatory Notes
[1]Perhaps for one of the festivals. [2]Isaiah 53:7–8.

Philip ... told him the good news about Jesus.

For Reflection
1. How did Philip meet the Ethiopian?
2. Explain the meaning of the passage the Ethiopian was reading.
3. What reason do those who know Jesus as their Savior have for being joyful?

Words to Remember

There is one body and one Spirit—just as you were called to one hope when you were called—one Lord, one faith, one baptism. *Ephesians 4:4–5*

Saul's Conversion

Acts 9

Meanwhile, Saul was still breathing out murderous threats[1] against the Lord's disciples. He went to the high priest and asked him for letters to the synagogues in Damascus, so that if he found any there who belonged to the Way,[2] he might take them as prisoners to Jerusalem.

As he neared Damascus, suddenly a light from heaven flashed around him. He fell to the ground and heard a voice say to him, "Saul, Saul, why do you persecute Me?"

"Who are You, Lord?" Saul asked.

"I am Jesus, whom you are persecuting," He replied. "Now get up and go into the city, and you will be told what you must do."

Saul got up from the ground, but when he opened his eyes he could see nothing. So the men traveling with him led him by hand into Damascus.

In Damascus there was a disciple named Ananias. The Lord called to him in a vision,[3] "Ananias! Go to the house of Judas and ask for a man from Tarsus named Saul, for he is praying. This man is My chosen instrument to carry My name before the Gentiles and their kings and before the people of Israel."

Then Ananias went to the house and entered it. Placing his hands on Saul, he said, "Brother Saul, the Lord Jesus has sent me so that you may see again and be filled with the Holy Spirit." Immediately, something like scales fell from Saul's eyes, and he could see again. He got up and was baptized.

Saul spent several days with the disciples in Damascus. At once he began to preach in the synagogues that Jesus is the Son of God. After many days had gone by, the Jews conspired to kill him. Day and night they kept close watch on the city gates, but his followers took him by night and lowered him in a basket through an opening in the wall. When he came to Jerusalem, he moved about freely in Jerusalem, speaking boldly in the name of the Lord.

Explanatory Notes

[1]He was fierce in persecuting and killing. [2]Believers in Christ. [3]The Lord appeared to him.

Suddenly a light from heaven flashed around him.

For Reflection

1. Describe Saul before and after Jesus came to claim him as His own.
2. Saul was blind both before and after Jesus spoke to Him. In what way were we like Saul in His blindness? In what way are we now able to see?
3. What special work did Jesus have for Saul to do? What special work does He have for you to do?

Words to Remember

Boldly and without hindrance he preached the kingdom of God and taught about the Lord Jesus Christ. *Acts 28:31*

Peter Is Freed from Prison

Acts 12

It was about this time that King Herod[1] arrested some who belonged to the church, intending to persecute them. When he saw that this pleased the Jews, he proceeded to seize Peter also.

So Peter was kept in prison, but the church was earnestly praying to God for him. The night before Herod was to bring him to trial, Peter was sleeping between two soldiers, bound with two chains, and sentries stood guard at the entrance. Suddenly an angel of the Lord appeared and a light shone in the cell. He struck Peter on the side and woke him up. "Quick, get up!" he said, and the chains fell off Peter's wrists. Then the angel said to him, "Put on your clothes and sandals." And Peter did so. "Wrap your cloak around you and follow me," the angel told him.

Peter followed him out of the prison, but he had no idea that what the angel was doing was really happening; he thought he was seeing a vision. They passed the first and second guards and came to the iron gate leading to the city. It opened for them by itself, and they went through it. When they had walked the length of one street, suddenly the angel left him.

Then Peter came to himself and said, "Now I know without a doubt that the Lord sent His angel and rescued me from Herod's clutches and from everything the Jewish people were anticipating."

When this had dawned on him, he went to the house of Mary the mother of John, also called Mark, where many people had gathered and were praying. Peter knocked at the outer entrance, and a servant girl named Rhoda came to answer the door. When she recognized Peter's voice, she was so overjoyed she ran back without opening it and exclaimed, "Peter is at the door!"

"You're out of your mind," they told her. When she kept insisting that it was so, they said, "It must be his angel." But Peter kept on knocking, and when they opened the door and saw him, they were astonished.

Peter motioned with his hand for them to be quiet and described how the Lord had brought him out of prison.

Explanatory Notes
[1]Herod Agrippa I, king of Judea (A.D.37–44), the grandson of Herod the Great.

Many people had gathered and were praying.

For Reflection

1. How did the members of the church respond after Peter was arrested?
2. Why did Rhoda not let Peter into the house?
3. For whom can you pray today?

Words to Remember

Do not be anxious about anything, but in everything, by prayer and petition, with thanksgiving, present your requests to God. *Philippians 4:6*

Paul's Shipwreck

Acts 27–28

When it was decided that we would sail for Italy, Paul and some other prisoners were handed over to a centurion named Julius. We boarded a ship and put out to sea.

Before very long, a wind of hurricane force, called the "northeaster," swept down from the island.[1] The ship was caught by the storm and could not head into the wind; so we gave way to it and were driven along. We took such a violent battering from the storm that the next day they[2] began to throw the cargo overboard.

When neither sun nor stars appeared for many days and the storm continued raging, we finally gave up all hope of being saved. After the men had gone a long time without food, Paul stood up before them and said: "Last night an angel of the God whose I am and whom I serve stood beside me and said, 'Do not be afraid, Paul. You must stand trial before Caesar; and God has graciously given you the lives of all who sail with you.' So keep up your courage, men, for I have faith in God that it will happen just as He told me."

When daylight came, they did not recognize the land, but they saw a bay with a sandy beach, where they decided to run the ship aground if they could. The soldiers planned to kill the prisoners to prevent any of them from swimming away and escaping. But the centurion wanted to spare Paul's life and kept them from carrying out their plan. He ordered those who could swim to jump overboard first and get to land. The rest were to get there on planks or on pieces of the ship. In this way everyone reached land in safety.

Once safely on shore, we found out that the island was called Malta.[3] The islanders showed us unusual kindness. They built a fire and welcomed us all because it was raining and cold. They honored us in many ways and when we were ready to sail, they furnished us with the supplies we needed.

Explanatory Notes
[1]Crete. [2]The passengers and crew. [3]A small island south of Sicily.

Everyone reached land in safety.

For Reflection

1. Paul was arrested and was on his way to be tried in Rome because he believed in Jesus. Tell about the adventure he encountered along the way.

2. Why wasn't Paul worried though a severe storm raged on around him?

3. Why can you have courage even as you face storms and troubles in your life?

Words to Remember

When I called, You answered me; You made me bold and stouthearted. *Psalm 138:3*